Drama Education in the Lives of Girls

Imagining Possibilities

Kathleen Gallagher

With a Foreword by Madeleine Grumet

UNIVERSITY OF TORONTO PRESS
Toronto Buffalo London

Printed in Canada

ISBN 0-8020-4763-7

∞

Printed on acid-free paper

Canadian Cataloguing in Publication Data

Gallagher, Kathleen, 1965–
   Drama education in the lives of girls : imagining possibilities

   Includes bibliographical references and index.
   ISBN 0-8020-4763-7

   1. Drama – Study and teaching (Secondary).   2. Teenage girls – education.
   I. Title.

PN1701.G34 2000   792'.071'2   C00-931198-X

This book has been published with the help of a grant from the Humanities and Social Sciences Federation of Canada, using funds provided by the Social Sciences and Humanities Research Council of Canada.

The University of Toronto Press acknowledges the financial assistance to its publishing program of the Canada Council for the Arts and the Ontario Arts Council.

University of Toronto Press acknowledges the financial support for its publishing activities of the Government of Canada through the Book Publishing Industry Development Program (BPIDP).

In loving memory of my parents,
Jean Rogers Gallagher and Edward Gallagher

Contents

Foreword by Madeleine Grumet ix

Acknowledgments xiii

Prologue 3

1. Drama and Girls 13

Reflection and Ethnography in Classrooms 13
Girls' Voices: The Conversations 18
Inviting the Aesthetic into Classrooms 21
Expanding the Question of Equity 28
Girls and Institutions: The Myth of Co-Education 30
Single-Sex Education: Beginning from 'Ourselves' 32
Our Setting 38

2. Creators of Worlds 43

Living through Stories 43
Drama and Expressive Learning 45
Dramatic Structures I 47
Drama and Intelligence 51
Spontaneous Role-Playing and Cognition 52
Change as a Significant Indicator of Cognitive
    Development 58
Drama and Moral Development 59

Dramatic Structures II 62
Drama as Collective Process 68
Drama as Personal Development 76

3. **Research in the Classroom** 85
Personal Narrative and Self-Construction 85
The 'Insider' Outside Eyes: Videographer Voices 97
Becoming a Teacher-Researcher 103
Assumptions and Paradigms: Three Propositions to
   Consider 105
The Importance of Evaluating the Arts in Schools 108

4. **Teacher Roles and the Curriculum** 113
The Drama Practitioner: Imagining Possibilities 113
Bringing the World In 115
The Action of Curriculum: When Objectives Meet
   Practice 119
The Problem of Goal-Setting in the Arts 121
The Projects of Drama are the Projects of Life 126

Epilogue 131

References 137

Index 151

Foreword

Many of us remember growing up in classrooms surrounded by scores of other people. Most were other students, maybe thirty or more, in public-school classrooms. Despite the numbers, the profusion, the jumble of kids, class proceeded as if we were all one student. That was the alchemy of the expert teacher, transforming a motley group of kids into a coherent unit. Desks were in rows, nailed down to the floor. Eyes front, everyone.

The sixties and seventies brought in an ethic of individuation, and a belated and often reluctant recognition of diversity. In teacher-centred classrooms, teachers were now exhorted to perceive and acknowledge the specific learning styles, needs, and attitudes of each of the thirty students, and to individualize the curriculum created for one generic child accordingly. One teacher and thirty students, maybe an aide. Schools were built without classrooms by visionaries who imagined mobile groups of children moving from learning centre to learning centre without categorization by age or grade. It was a romantic idea that nobody was prepared for. The curriculum and the structures of instruction changed little. There was little material developed for this fluid curriculum, less pedagogy, and even less assessment. Gradually, amid the din and the distraction, bookcases appeared, and the walls grew back to establish the cubicles that would order and focus attention on – the teacher.

The eighties and nineties brought a stronger learning theory to this scene, as constructivism, born of Piaget's conviction that

symbol formation required activity as well as ideation, began to inform learning theory in mathematics and science. Nevertheless, the task of shaping learning experiences, so that children are able to discover what we want them to know, is very complex and subtle work. Too often, particularly in mathematics and sciences, constructivism founders on the shoals of the one right answer.

Unlike the sciences, the humanities do not seek the discovery of natural or logical laws. In literature, philosophy, history, political science, it is possible, even desirable, to ask a question and receive many – often contradictory – answers. The task of a democracy, as Kathleen Gallagher argues in this book, is to both provoke and encourage this proliferation of opinions, and at the same time provide a process that can incorporate them, bringing them into relation to each other.

The drama work that Kathleen Gallagher describes in this book provides a model for a constructivist curriculum in the humanities. In her hands this work is simultaneously differentiated and active because the knowledge that is its goal is constructed through performance by each participating student. Even more important, the knowledge that is its goal is necessarily specific to the participants. In this work there is no one right answer, as is still the case in so many of the so-called constructivist curricula. What Kathleen Gallagher's students learn is to imagine, to feel, and to advocate ideas that are different from their own. As this process unfolds, one is impressed throughout with the compassion it engenders. Now the 'others' in the classroom, ignored for centuries, are a source of knowledge, achieved through imagination and relation.

In this text we also get a glimpse of the kind of teaching this work requires. Because it is not driving to the right answer with that relentless rhythm of sequential and tested curriculum, the question to be asked about an action, Gallagher tells us, is not *what happens next*, but *what happens when*. She slows the work down, creating exercises and improvisations that ask students to tumble off the linear curriculum so that they can explore all the ramifications of the problem they are studying. Weaving

together the theory of John Dewey and Paolo Freire with the art of Jonathan Neelands, Cecily O'Neil, David Booth, Dorothy Heathcote, and Gavin Bolton, Gallagher brings us, along with her students, through the doors and corridors of imagination and reason. She is justly proud of her teachers, her students, and her own work.

Among the many insights into her work that Gallagher provides is her statement that the teacher of drama must be both inside and outside the work. In that phrase she captures the tension, and pleasure, of brilliant teaching. In the old days we were only inside the work, curled in its phrases, circling its history and structures. Recently, we have been too far outside the work, concerned about skill acquisition and process, losing the texture and specificity of substance. Teachers, Kathleen Gallagher tells us, must 'be passionate about more than their teaching. They will then bring their passions and their commitments to their teaching, and infuse their work with the creativity of their whole lives.' Clearly, Kathleen Gallagher is a teacher with this double vision and presence.

She works with the 'as if' gesture that situates the actual moment as just one instance of the possible as necessary to art, to teaching, and to democracy. She recognizes other people not only as they are but as they might be. She celebrates their subjectivity as well as their presence and extends a greeting to the fullest expression of their humanity. And so she demonstrates the necessity for making art in education.

MADELEINE GRUMET

Acknowledgments

I could not begin, in a few short paragraphs, to acknowledge all the people in my life to whom I owe my gratitude. Still, I would like to pay homage to two worlds. First, to the university where my ideas have been nurtured and challenged, where my mind has been engaged over many years. I have had the privilege of completing a doctoral degree in education at the Ontario Institute for Studies in Education of the University of Toronto. Over these years, I have met and studied with some exceptional scholars, too many to name. But I am particularly grateful to David Booth, my inspiring and supportive supervisor, who continues to keep me laughing, as well as Howard Russell, Ruth Roach Pierson, and Johan Aitken, who, early on, showed a genuine interest in my work and continued to support me in fundamental ways. I have been engrossed by the communion of minds that this place and these people have come to represent for me.

Over the past few years, I have also had the opportunity to travel to many different parts of this country and abroad, and have met a passionate, international group of teacher educators, arts educators, and feminists who have expanded, in important ways, the academic community of which I am proud to be a part. For her insights, I would especially like to thank Madeleine Grumet.

Second, I must recognize St Jude's College School, where teacher-colleagues have represented a communion of hearts, committed to caring for and educating young women. My

school, as schools can be, was a nurturing community over some ten years. But here, I owe the greatest debt of gratitude to my students – the grade 10s – strong young women whose questions have challenged me throughout my teaching career, and whose voices have guided my writing of this book. They have allowed me to know more fully the unique and imaginative aspects of identity and agency in their school lives and opened up for discussion the complex and contradictory nature of their adolescent selves. They have set me on my life projects. My profound admiration extends also to the four senior drama students – now university students – who videotaped my classroom events over many months and whose insights were indispensable to me.

I am deeply grateful to my family for their continued support and love, and to my friends for ongoing dialogues about what matters. I am especially indebted to Beth Mairs and John Gilbert for their wisdom, constancy, and love.

I know that my life would not be as rich and rewarding if I had not enjoyed the support, gentleness, and boundless love of my parents. Both taken too young, and before I could share with them all that I wanted to share, this book is for them.

DRAMA EDUCATION IN THE LIVES OF GIRLS

Imagining Possibilities

Drama: A Picture of Our Knowing

Aphra: When a woman marries, she becomes a femme covert. Her legal exist-
ence is made inseparable from her husband's. Not just her property, her very
existence. She is – covered. I've always remembered that. The covered woman.
The masked woman. (Pause) Betty, I think – If I were to write my woman's
tragedy now, I think it would be – silent. No words at all. And that silence
would hold all the voices that never speak, of all the women who are never
heard. Covered women who live and die and leave no history behind except a
few lines on a tombstone. Wife of. Sister to. Daughter. Widow. Four possibili-
ties, no more. And even in death our stories are written by someone else.

Beth Herst, 'A Woman's Comedy' (1991)

The illustrious Mrs Aphra Behn, living in the seventeenth century, was the first woman in England to earn her living as a professional writer, and one of the first women writers to refuse to
adopt a male pseudonym. Despite the bleak outlook of her
'woman's tragedy,' she indeed resisted boundaries and imagined other worlds.

This book is about imagining other worlds. It will explore
what drama can be, and often is, for girls. With the perceptions
and voices of girls in a publicly funded, heterogeneous, urban,
single-sex school as my steady guide throughout, I hope this
book will shed new light on familiar questions – questions concerning gender and equity in education. And, just as important,
it will add strong classroom-based evidence to a growing body

of research in drama education – evidence of the aesthetic, social, and academic advantages of a drama curriculum – and significantly advance the theory/practice conversation.

In secondary education in Ontario, Canada, the dramatic arts represent a subject discipline that falls within the larger field known as *the arts*. What the drama curriculum shares with the other arts (visual arts, dance, music) in high schools is the value placed on students' creativity and imagination and on their active participation in the learning processes. In other words, the arts depart from the more traditional styles of instruction and learning, both in their organization and their evaluation mechanisms.

While all the arts involve some measure of self-exploration, the dramatic arts also invite students to enter into the intimate learning processes of their classmates. Walter Pitman's (1998) recent work on the arts in Canada and in Canadian schools describes the capacity of the arts to give meaning to the rest of the school curriculum. Despite this unifying and integrating function of the arts in schools, however, there still remains a hierarchy of knowledge that places the measurable and objective subjects at the top, leaving the experiential and subjective at the bottom (212). Over his many years of observation of Canadian schools, Pitman concludes that there continues to be a perception of the arts as 'play,' entertainment, a kind of relaxation at the end of the day. Yet, he adds:

> arts education programs in some schools are rigorous. They stretch the mind and the emotional capacity of the student. In good arts education classes there is a seriousness, an intensity that is a wonder to behold. This quality can sometimes be experienced by attending a play, a musical or a concert in the local school gymnasium. Even during those mythical years of the '70s and '80s, when it was assumed that excellence had disappeared from the classrooms of North America entirely, the quality of music or drama at such events left the adult audience in awe. Yet arts classes are still viewed as unimportant. (51)

I have always found it curious that in schools (and most mark-

edly in high schools) drama is considered a 'lightweight' subject, soft, of the emotions – in essence, *for girls*. Drama is a gendered subject, not masculine like maths and sciences, which are hard, of the mind, *not for girls*. Despite countless examples of the power of drama in the lives of both girls and boys, its stigma as lacking weight and seriousness prevails. This view of drama as frill is particularly prevalent in Western educational thought, but in other parts of the world, drama is not to be taken lightly. When drama articulates the voice of the people, as in the case, for instance, of Augusto Boal's theatre of the oppressed in South America or the Market Theatre of Johannesburg in South Africa, drama is indeed powerful and threatening for it can expose and challenge existing structures and effect change.

For Scottish writer, director, and producer John McGrath (1981), theatre is the most public and most clearly political of the art forms:

> Theatre is the place where the life of a society is shown in public to that society, where that society's assumptions are exhibited and tested, its values are scrutinized, its myths are validated and its traumas become emblems of its reality. Theatre is not about the reaction of one sensibility to events external to itself, as poetry tends to be; or the private consumption of fantasy or a mediated slice of social reality, as most novels tend to be. It is a public event, and it is about matters of public concern. (83)

McGrath explores the power of theatre work by taking up issues of audience, class, and form. He deviates from a liberal arts perspective in his argument for the dialectical and inclusive potential of theatre. Its ability to 'humanize,' he argues, lies in enlarging the concept of 'human' in a dialectical manner. This ability of theatre to mediate reality ensures its active intervention in forming contemporary life and contributing to the future of society. I would suggest that it is this tradition of theatre that has significantly influenced drama education, for *process drama* (Cecily O'Neill, 1995) is about both the personal and collective concerns and experiences of the group.

I have observed the many ways in which girls' work in educational drama can create opportunities for them to interrupt the limited and limiting discourses and possibilities assigned to them in schools. Drama asks them to mediate reality by working with metaphor, analogy, and symbolism, and, most significantly, it asks girls to speak their own understandings of the world. Evelyn, a grade 10 drama student, explained to me one day why she thought she was 'different' in drama class:

> In drama I'm more outspoken. I don't know ... this class doesn't really feel like a class. It just feels like ... like you're teaching me new things and I'm just exploring it. It doesn't feel ... I don't feel, like, you know ... straight. Usually like in math and science there's a way you have to act. You can't express yourself ... freely. I mean sometimes you show really high feelings or what you think about and sometimes you just, like, see things in your environment. I don't know, drama just brings out that.

In the following pages, I shall explain why I am strongly persuaded that when students do drama they are engaged in a profoundly educational experience. The arts help both to impassion students and to recover their lost intensity. While I would not suggest that drama necessarily teaches anyone how to 'act,' I do think that it often helps students overcome those things that inhibit them from participating in fictional play. And for girls this means the freedom to construct themselves outside prescribed roles, to be like Aphra Behn and imagine other worlds.

The roles teachers play in students' learning and in their lives is central to our understanding of education as the 'practice of freedom,' in the words of bell hooks (1994a). It is not that our freedom lies in the hands of great teachers, but that great teachers undergird our dreams of freedom, our possibilities.

My greatest teacher was my father. My father considered teaching a truly noble profession. He would have made a great teacher himself, but he had not enjoyed the privilege of higher education and, in pre-war Scotland, was encouraged to learn a trade. Nonetheless, he remained a 'life-long' learner and, once in

Canada, enrolled in every adult education course available to him. As is the case in many immigrant families, education was greatly prized in our family. When I decided to become a teacher, he congratulated me on choosing the 'best profession in the world.'

But it was neither his respect for the profession nor his thirst for knowledge that made the greatest marks on me. Instead, it was his very life that taught me what I have come to value as the two most important qualities a teacher can possess: I learned from his example that a teacher must envision a world of possibilities; and I learned that a teacher is a caregiver, in the fullest sense of the word. While there are many other virtues one may assign the 'good teacher,' these have remained the hallmarks for me.

I would like to recall a significant story about my father. And thinking about him means remembering my 'daughter-self.' I was 12 years old when my father read, in our community newspaper, about a new baseball league that was about to begin in the east end of Toronto. It announced a registration date for kids between the ages of 11 and 17 at the local community centre. My father asked me if I would like to play and I thought I might. He took me along to register, but when we arrived, the baseball convenors kindly explained that it was a hardball league, the implication clearly being *not for girls*.

They explained to my father that there were several softball leagues in the area that I might like to join. Referring to the newspaper clipping in his hand, my father persisted, indicating that their advertisement invited 'kids' to play baseball. They delicately explained further that, despite having advertised the league that way, it would be evident to anyone that it meant boys when they saw that it was a hardball league. I remember feeling a little embarrassed that my father still did not seem to 'get it.' Even I understood that hardball was for boys. At that point, he turned to me and asked whether I would like to play hardball. Somewhat confused, but rather instinctively, I nodded 'yes' and my father turned back and looked blankly at the chaps behind the desk. I was very aware that they seemed irritated, but to my surprise they looked at each other and then turned to

us and one of them said, 'Well she can try it if you like, but I don't think she'll enjoy herself.' My father turned to me again and asked if I'd like to play baseball. I gave a definitive 'yes!' We signed the forms and picked out a uniform; I could hardly wait until my first game.

In the first year, I was the only girl in the league; the next year there were two others. Today, when I drive by the park where I used to play – in the diamond under the big stadium lights – I smile because half of the players on the field are girls. And like me, these girls don't 'throw like girls' because they are expected to throw strongly and skilfully. I am grateful now, in many circumstances, that I don't 'throw like a girl,' but I am more grateful that my father wanted to realize a different world for me – a world of possibilities – a world where girls play hardball too.

As I think back, I also remember the greatest worry of my childhood: the fragility of my mother's health. My mother suffered tremendous pain in her life. She had chronic back pain and severe medical conditions that limited her life in many ways. From a very early age, I remember always carrying with me the fear of my mother's death. It was my single greatest worry. Nonetheless, she lived as fully as she could with her back pain, her cardiovascular disease, her amputated leg. It was finally cancer that took her life. Through the twenty-nine years of my life that she lived, I cannot recall her being without pain. Yet I knew a quiet and joyful woman who cherished the support and loving care of her husband. My father was her caregiver for as long as I can remember. He was at her side when she rallied back from operations. And as the cancer took its hold in increasingly terrible ways, he stood by her during treatments, bearing pictures of her – smiling, in better days – so the doctors would never lose sight of the person they were treating. In the final year of her life, my father was also struck with cancer and died in a very short six weeks. I had learned the role of caregiver well from him. We all had. And so my three sisters, my brother, and I cared for them both until their deaths, only nine months apart. Theirs was the greatest love story I had known; their deaths, the most unimaginable and tragic loss.

I have learned many things from this bereavement in my life. I am constantly filled with their presence. For my mother, the glass was always half-full, where tomorrow might prove to be a better day. Her grace and steadfastness remain with me. For my father, it was his role as caregiver, until his own death, that was his greatest legacy. He was a man who embodied the courage, vision, and sheer intelligence of his working-class ancestors. From both of them I learned that good teachers show love and enjoy abundant love in return.

This is a book for teachers: those in schools, those preparing to be in schools, and those who help in new teachers' preparation for the awesome task awaiting them. Since teachers, as the greatest sources of reflection and analysis of classroom actions, are the real key to sustainable curriculum reform and progress in education, it is my special wish that this book might help ignite the reflective spectators within us and inspire conversations about the place of creativity and reflection in teaching.

It has often been said that much of teaching is intuitive, based on the insights and receptivity of teachers in their particular contexts. Teaching, then, is about specificity, the interactions of particular persons in particular locations at a given time. When I began my Ph.D. research, I was teaching in a single-sex, Catholic secondary school for girls. Over three semesters, as a teacher in this context, I began videotaping all my drama classes (there were five over the one and a half years of my taping) at the grade 10 level. I explained to my students that I wanted us to reflect on what we were doing together in drama. They were very keen to embark on this project. Steinburg and Kincheloe (1998) consider that students are 'experts' about their own lives and needs and can be viewed as researchers themselves. I have generally found that adolescents are interested in making life significant, particulary because there is often pressure to behave as though it were tedious and uninteresting. Adolescents are supportive and honest when they believe that the adult world is taking them seriously. My work has also convinced me that serious reflection on their actions in the classroom can strengthen students' engagement in their learning experiences. Using this

reflective-practitioner approach to my multi-case study of drama practices in early adolescence, I came to think about how this kind of systematic reflection on the actions of teaching and learning provides two advantages: It allows us to depart from the more traditional, results-oriented kind of classroom negotiation and helps us to move into a more growth-oriented approach to teaching.

To better understand how my students in these five drama classes were negotiating their learning, I needed first to broaden my own understanding of adolescent girls. Turning to the vast literature on girls and education, I began by examining many of the challenges that girls historically have faced in schools. As an equity-centred teacher, when I decided to formally study the culture of girls I was working with, I did so with the explicit intention of identifying those aspects of their schooling that might be inhibiting their full participation in their learning, as well as those aspects that enhance educational experiences and outcomes. While curriculum needs and pedagogical concerns are particular to specific contexts, I expect that my observations might also enhance the general curriculum choices and pedagogical considerations of teachers in diverse contexts. Moreover, I invited my students to speak their experiences of schooling and equity in a Canadian urban context at the end of the twentieth century. Girls' stories both inside the classroom and in interviews taught me about many of the ways girls make sense – and often take charge – of their learning.

Chapter 1, 'Drama and Girls,' sets the backdrop of the single-sex classroom where I taught and addresses some of the pressing questions for all of us concerning equity in public education. Chapter 2, 'Creators of Worlds,' describes in detail the stories we built in our dramas, including the girls' own descriptions of their learning in/through dramatic role-play. Of course, doing drama is a very particular kind of school activity. The drama we did together was largely improvised, that is, scriptless and spontaneously created. This kind of contextualized classroom drama is often used to explore social issues, literature, and personal narratives. Drama's goals, then, are affective, scholarly, and

artistic. The videotaped hours of my classes helped me to capture these layers of learning often taking place within the magic of improvised theatre. Chapter 3, 'Research in the Classroom,' describes my own model as a reflective practitioner, illustrating how I listened to the stories of my students' classroom experiences. Chapter 4, 'Teacher Roles and the Curriculum,' examines the crucial role teachers play in children's learning and contemplates the creative and challenging task of developing curriculum and assessing learning in the arts.

This book, which grew out of my original Ph.D. research, now has three particular purposes. First, both my observations and the girls' own descriptions of their classroom experiences will add to our ever-changing understanding of girlhood, that period of adolescence where the simpler certainties of childhood and the ambiguities of adulthood meet head on. Second, by sharing my own journey as a reflective practitioner, I offer the hope for meaningful reflection on practice for teachers in an increasingly mechanistic, functional, and disempowering period in education. Teachers must again have a real stake in curriculum reform; learning from one's own practice is, I am convinced, the most critical starting place. Having a personal stake in classroom research does not disqualify that research. Research generated from teachers' classrooms by teachers themselves has the potential to redefine what counts as research. And finally, by sharing my students' performances of understanding, their aesthetic investigations and prodigious imaginations, I will make my particular contribution to the growing evidence of drama's ability to animate the processes of learning.

Chapter One

Drama and Girls

The wind of tradition is a chill wind, because it brings a message of exclusion
– stay out; because it brings a message of subordination – stay under; because
it brings a message of objectification – become the object of another's worship
or desire, see yourself as you have been seen for centuries through a male gaze.
And because all of the suffering, the endless litany of storm and shipwreck is
presented as necessary or even good for civilization, the message to women is:
keep quiet and notice the absence of women and say nothing.

Carol Gilligan, 'Teaching Shakespeare's Sister:
Notes from the Underground of Female Adolescence' (1990)

Reflection and Ethnography in Classrooms

Researching in one's own classroom requires a teacher to think
explicitly about how one listens to and reflects upon one's students. Nancie Atwell (1987), a teacher-researcher who investi-
gated writing, reading, and learning with adolescents, explains
that teacher research is not a secret we keep from students for
fear of skewing our findings. Instead, it is a model for our students of how adults can function as life-long learners and of
learning as a social activity. She believes that when teachers
invite students to become partners in inquiry, to collaborate with
them in wondering about what, and how, they are learning,
schools become more 'thoughtful' places.

Ethnography is critical in drama research because it can capture the process of classroom action and the spontaneity of

reflection. Taylor (1996) describes ethnography as research that 'demands an understanding of how people think, feel, and act within their own naturalistic settings' (37). Videotaping our drama stories and open-ended discussions and interviews, as well as engaging the reflection of those 'outside' our stories (the videographers), allowed me to listen to important evolving talk from insiders and outsiders about their own and the group's experiences in/through drama. Without question, ethnographic research methods have brought participants in education studies into the centre of inquiry. They have helped us understand, in the broadest possible terms, not the objects of scientific inquiry, but the processes themselves. The data, formerly the sole source for meaning-making and explanations, are now a part of the larger research picture that includes the insights of the subjects who are their source. In many cases, the reflections and perspectives of subjects in the research act are an essential part of the negotiation of meaning. It would seem that the reporting of research data no longer need happen in a vacuum and can include, in important ways, the subjects who speak in different registers and from diverse vantage points. Burdell and Swadener (1999) call it an emerging genre in educational scholarship – critical personal narrative and autoethnography in education – seeing it as educational theory that foregrounds the personal while not evading the complex and contradictory nature of theory and research.

My research as a reflective practitioner operated with the assumption that realities are manifold and truths are provisional. The term 'reflective practitioner' turns research, with connotations of outside evaluators and recognized wisdom, on its head, for it entails a valuing of teachers' practical and tacit knowing. This often leads to practitioners thinking about their own thinking, as Maxine Greene (1991) points out. The practices of reflective practice and action research, for instance, are designed to make the work of classroom teachers visible and central to the problem of understanding how teaching and learning can be made more effective (Neelands, 1996). Teachers are the guardians of education. Booth and Wells (1994), in their

work, propose 'communities of inquiry' in which teachers might both initiate research and have a greater voice in educational decision-making. This model provides opportunities for collaboration between university-based researchers and classroom-based teacher-researchers. The more differently positioned eyes there are, the more complete the picture.

The groundbreaking work of Donald Schon (1983) and his discussions of 'reflection-in-action' have had enormous influence on reflective practitioners. For example, the 'reflection-in-action' process, in which a teacher who cannot get a point across and then suddenly hears differently what the students are saying, is referred to by Schon as a 'reframing.' Reframing results when teachers respond to puzzles arising within their teaching actions and in the relationship between beliefs and actions (Russell and Munby, 1991). Anderson and Herr (1999), arguing for the place of rigorous practitioner knowledge in schools and universities, explain:

> We could argue that insider researchers have unique opportunities to document the hidden transcripts within social institutions, illuminating new forms of micropolitics and an institutional dimension only partially accessible to researchers ... One might suggest that insider researchers have access similar to those researchers who go underground, operating daily over a period of years in the school, in multiple roles, one of which being that of researcher. (18–19)

While serious ethical questions about so-called 'underground' research clearly exist, it is indisputable that teachers in their multitude of roles in schools and in children's lives have access to worlds unknown to the 'outsider.'

I see the inevitable relationship of the teacher-researcher to the subjects as an advantage that allows for greater depth of analysis, given the more complete understanding of the participants and the practice of the discipline the teacher-researcher brings to the data. Also, given the nature of drama and the kinds of personal discoveries students often make, familiarity with the

teacher can make it easier for students to describe their experiences and feelings, particularly when the teacher-researcher has been part of the process, as in participant-observation modes of inquiry. Wolcott (1990, 133) refers to his researcher stance as 'rigorous subjectivity,' opting for a subjectivity that strengthens qualitative approaches rather than an objectivity that may be neither possible nor desirable.

It is important to clarify the importance of the privileged position of the 'insider' in drama work. The teacher seldom evaluates the work only from the outside, because she is also a participant, often in a role, inside the work. The videographers of our classroom activities, however, witnessed the work but did not participate in it, retaining some critical distance and neutrality as far as the students were concerned.

Finally, it is the explanations of the students themselves that assure a negotiation of meaning in my retelling of their stories. Their understanding of drama conventions, the worlds they create, and the implications of this work in their lives is the best assurance of a kind of 'researcher distance' in my accounts. Admittedly, it is my belief that drama does challenge students to work in different and often intensified ways. But I especially wanted to find out whether this kind of curriculum can allow for growth and change in the way that students perceive themselves and their peers in their experience of schooling.

My interviews with the grade 10 drama students, the videotaping of drama lessons, and the videographer questionnaire provided the greatest sources of data collected over the two school years. This triangulation, or use of a variety of methods, also guards against a narrow view of the study site. The video recording approach, however imperfect and incomplete, was integral to the design of the research because it captured the process of the work and allowed me to review those lessons in which I was involved deeply as participant and facilitator of the class. Re-seeing the classroom events brought back the feelings of doing the work even when the details began to fade. The video can never recapture the entirety of the event, in the same way that a play that is documented remains incomplete, merely

seen through one lens. But the videotaping did allow me to reflect on those ephemeral moments, once removed from the rawness of the actual events.

I kept detailed notes, which included people's own words as well as summaries of conversations and events in the classroom. The videographer questionnaire was completed after the study and asked the informed 'outside eyes' – the four senior students who had videotaped the classroom dramas – to reflect on the work they had witnessed. Further, these students were asked to consider their own experiences of grade 10 drama and reflect on these experiences through the lens of retrospection. These young women's insights about the study brought differently positioned and important perspectives to the work we had done. They also suggested areas for further research in their comprehensive reflections about their own past experiences of drama in a single-sex school. With all these rich 'data,' I was still troubled over how to respeak their stories. What I had been was a witness of their telling. But I am clearly more 'insider' than 'outsider,' and I had to work hard to uncover the taken-for-granted assumptions of my own practice.

Participant observation is a very natural stance for teachers because it is already both implicit and explicit in our daily work. Teachers are asked regularly to assess and evaluate students (in report cards, for instance) and situations, with description that substantiates their observations. With participant observation as a method, we are carrying out these duties in a conscious and deliberate way. Participant observation allows researchers in education to place individuals centrally and focus on context, culture, and history. Practitioners regularly record what children say and do, thereby constructing their own understandings about the social realities of classrooms. Freire (1998b) insisted that there was no such thing as teaching without research and research without teaching. He explains:

> One inhabits the body of the other. As I teach, I continue to search and re-search. I teach because I search, because I question, and because I submit myself to questioning. I research because I notice

things, take cognizance of them. And in so doing, I intervene. And intervening, I educate and educate myself. I do research so as to know what I do not yet know and to communicate and proclaim what I discover. (35)

Teachers are well positioned, therefore, to conduct rich ethnographic studies of their work in classrooms and become students of their own teaching.

Why, one might easily ask, should teachers work so hard at a time when their contributions and expertise are minimized? Because it is the most powerful way to reclaim the vocation of teaching and a most compelling and rewarding act. If theory is a search for reasons why things are as they are – what Freire (1998a) has described as 'thinking the practice' – then this kind of reflection on classroom practice, carried out by teachers, is key to understanding how to negotiate with significance, as Heathcote (1984b) has said, and involve students in high-quality endeavours.

Girls' Voices: The Conversations

The interviews I conducted with the students occurred, in each case, at the end of the semester, to allow some time and distance from the experiences to mediate reflection. They aimed to understand the students' sense of self and sense of the group. Our dialogue began inside the drama work, between teacher and student, and among students themselves. The interviews, then, were a natural extension of the kinds of questions and insights the girls had experienced during the course. The questions invited them to make explicit and, in some cases, piece together the thoughts and insights they had during the drama work. Further to this, they encouraged the students, based on their experience, to speculate on drama work in contexts other than the single-sex one they knew. The interview, in other words, was not simply interested in substantiating or rejecting previously formulated hypotheses.

Five questions served as a guideline for our discussions:

1. Why did you take drama?
2. Do you see yourself as different in this class as compared with your other classes?
3. Do you think there are characteristics or aspects of yourself and your life experiences that you brought into the dramas we worked on together?
4. Are there other areas of school where you think your personal/cultural experiences are included or important?
5. Do you think being in a classroom of all girls makes a difference in how you work in class?

The semi-structured, open-ended form of the interviews, in many cases, however, became an open discussion between teacher and student within a safe and shared context, a negotiation of meanings with the subjects who are themselves the sources of the data. The interviews thus charted the terrain we (teacher-researcher and students) had covered together.

In their writing, feminist scholars have long privileged the place of women's own narratives, of women's different 'experience.' Teaching drama has convinced me of the paramount importance of experience and articulating one's experience in learning. So it is to the girls that I turned. To this I added my external observations of their experiences, as they shared – in their own words – the 'interiority' of their lived experience in a single-sex drama class.

It was not possible to interview all 139 girls, and so I asked for volunteers who would be interested in being interviewed in a more formal way. From within the five grade 10 classes, there emerged a self-selected group of nineteen girls who wanted to discuss, in greater depth, their experiences in our classroom. Here, I found Brown and Gilligan's (1992) work with adolescent girls very useful. They described a 'Listener's Guide' in their approach to the interviewing of adolescent girls, in a longitudinal study undertaken by the Harvard Project on Women's Psychology and Girls' Development. Here, the 'resisting listener' must listen for and against conventions of relationship within a society and culture rooted, psychologically, in the experiences of

men. In this way, the listener enables relationship by taking in another's voice – the 'who is speaking, in what body, telling what story of relationship – from whose perspective, in what societal and cultural frameworks' (28).

Of the nineteen girls I interviewed, eighteen were from working-class homes with varying degrees of economic stability, including, for some, periods of family unemployment. One student was from a middle-class home. All nineteen participants were able-bodied. Fourteen of the girls were taking the majority of their courses in the advanced-level stream (now called Academic), two at the general-level stream (now called Applied); two were labelled with learning disabilities and one as 'gifted.' I should point out, however, that there was a strong trend in the school to study at the advanced-level stream and that these groupings are far less homogeneous than one might expect.

Of the nineteen participants, sixteen were first-generation Canadian (six of Portuguese heritage, five of Afro-Caribbean heritage, one of Southeast Asian heritage, one of Ukrainian heritage, one of Filipino heritage, one of Chinese heritage, and one of Italian heritage). The remaining three participants were new Canadians, having immigrated to Canada as children (one from the Philippines, one from Portugal, and one from Peru). This group of volunteers is very representative of the diversity found in this and many other inner-city schools. The excerpts of their personal narratives that I include in Chapter 3 come from all nineteen girls in their private, individual interviews with me.

Paolo Freire's (1998b) assumption is that the learner is 'unfinished' and knowing consists of the learner's capacity to situate herself in her own historicity, to grasp the class, race, and sexual aspects of education and social formation and to understand the complexities of the relations that have produced this situation. In Aronowitz' introduction to Freire's last work before his death in 1997, he eloquently describes Freire's position on learning. It has strong resonances for educational drama because it speaks to the agency of the learner upon which drama education rests. It is this experience of agency that my students frequently described in the interviews.

Inviting the Aesthetic into Classrooms

The experience of doing in education cannot be underestimated. At the beginning of this century, Dewey (1934) called for experiences in education, realizing that it is through returning to the most common experiences that we discover the aesthetic quality such experiences possess. Many years later, Kaufman (1971, 94) claimed that the arts provide the means of transforming feelings, sensations, and ideas into perceptible yet critically qualitative forms of understanding. More recently still, Karen Gallas (1994), who is researching the importance of narrative as a source of knowledge for children, looks to the artist in society as the person best able to tap into processes of thinking and communication that lie dormant in most of us from lack of use. She holds that children lose their natural gifts for narrative expression over years spent with adults, who are less flexible in their thinking and communication. She argues that children's entire education should provide opportunities for them to expand, rather than narrow, their range of expressive narrative functions.

Doing drama is a process, often simultaneously involving a loss and a discovery of realities, as students respond to abstractions or fictional worlds. The 'aesthetic' sensibility in drama embraces human images of beauty and horror. Charles Fowler (1994, 8), in his article 'Strong Arts, Strong Schools,' suggests that the arts put us in touch with our own and other people's feelings, teaching one of the great civilizing capacities: how to be empathetic. And the extent to which the arts teach empathy, they also develop our capacity for humaneness. Teachers of adolescents are often heard lamenting the 'diseases' of teenagers: complacency and indifference. It is, unfortunately, years of being schooled that have helped to numb the students' curiosity and vitality.

Sometimes, critical episodes in teaching can illuminate practice in new and often satisfying ways. One such incident in my classroom life – a Remembrance Day performance – crystallized many of the preoccupations I had as a teacher of the arts in a

single-sex school for girls. It illustrated, at once, three important principles that have since guided my teaching and created an imperative in my research work. I have learned that girls' knowledge is unique and uniquely articulated by them. I have learned that the collective process of doing drama can be a deeply human and humanizing process. And I have learned that inviting the 'aesthetic' into the classroom can give external form to the often subjugated inner lives of students.

The richness of these experiences in classrooms often invites us to probe further. I would like to recount one such experience. It is the story of a Remembrance Day project I embarked on with my students that began as a classroom exploration and ended in a theatrical production. This experience is one example that supports Fowler's (1994) view of the arts:

> The arts provide a more comprehensive and insightful education because they invite students to explore the emotional, intuitive, and irrational aspects of life that science is hard pressed to explain. Humans invented each of the arts as a fundamental way to represent aspects of reality; to try to make sense of the world, manage life better, and share these perceptions with others. The arts therefore enrich the curriculum by extending awareness and comprehension while affirming the interconnectedness of all forms of knowing. This is why an education without the arts is an incomplete education. (9)

The experience I am about to describe stands in sharp contrast to a co-educational classroom experience of another teacher who became interested in gender questions as a result of his experiences in the classroom. John Elliot (1974) had chosen 'war' as a topic for study in his classroom. He soon became very disturbed by the lack of female participation in his classroom. He tried to use his authority to open up the discussion and encourage the girls to speak. This was met with the ridicule of the boys because this was 'their' topic; they were the ones who spoke with authority. Girls, they thought, did not know about war. This does not mean that sex-role stereotypes and stereotypical

responses are the problem of co-educational settings alone. But these learned responses can be challenged and problematized differently in single-sex settings, which are often more conducive to challenging dichotomous thinking.

As a starting point for the preparation of our Remembrance Day performance, together we listened to Canadian singer John McDermott's recordings of old, mostly Irish and Scottish, war tunes. We heard the stories of men going to war, not returning from war, victories and defeats. Of the thirty-three students, only one was of British descent. The questions that followed and the story-telling the students performed seemed to somehow transcend both culture and gender while being firmly rooted in both these contexts. Through their explorations, they began to make the story their own. Each day, there seemed to be a growing sensitivity in the room. The horrors of war and lost lives were beginning to take the students outside their own context. They were beginning to see beyond themselves.

This sensitivity grew out of the stories and poems we read, the music we listened to, the tableaux we made, but mostly out of the stories we created. I soon realized that the students were beginning to understand certain things because they were finding their questions. These preliminary 'activities' – listening to music and lyrics, sharing family stories of war, looking through historical picture books – helped them form these questions. Had I simply asked them to tell me what they would like to understand about war, I believe the responses may have been more superficial. Drama leads to inquiry and, in the best scenario, passionate inquiry. The students were interested in knowing how people coped with separation in wartime. They also wanted to get at the heart of questions of patriotism. But most apparent was their interest in bringing these events out of the distant past and finding meaning within their current understanding of the world. Drama provides a framework that asks students to deepen and clarify possible ways of representing a theme or issue of concern. Out of this kind of exploration comes a product that is rethought and reshaped until it is dramatically satisfying.

What resulted for this group was an exceptional Remembrance Day performance. I had expected their sense of satisfaction to be great, having observed their process over two weeks, but I could not have anticipated the audience's response during the Remembrance Day service. It was at this time that the rather artificial distinction between drama (about the learner) and theatre (about communicating with an audience) – as if these two objectives were mutually exclusive – disappeared. Drama is exploration and performance; it is about the performer, the spectator, and the spectator within the performer. It also became clear that while arts teachers might spend a good deal of time 'packaging' programs to 'sell' their importance, nothing speaks louder and more plainly of our worth than our ability to look passionately at our own world through art. Malcolm Ross (1984) explains that we, in the arts, are understood as approaching the world from a poetic point of view. What remains, then, is to demonstrate that we are properly equipped to work in this way and that the children we are teaching are gaining poetic access to truths they value and that are of some objective significance. If our inner life is granted an external expression in an artistic endeavour, then we have not created something extraordinary but, rather, have allowed for the ordinary of our lives to be engaged.

Inviting the aesthetic into classrooms has a further benefit. In my experience, and certainly this was true for our Remembrance Day performance, students have a deeply rooted sense of the value of their work when it originates from them. In response to the question I put to the class after their performance – In working on the Remembrance Day performance, what qualities (yours, others', mine ...) made the process so productive and engaging? – Sandra answered:

> We all wanted to make the performance a success and show everyone what great actors we are. We wanted the performance to be special, so we all tried our best to make sure the audience felt what we were trying to show them. We worked together and performed not only to please the audience, but also ourselves.

Yolanda spoke of her sense of the power of the collectivity in drama:

> Coming in every morning knowing that everyone in the class would be working altogether on the same project was good to know. Listening to everyone's different ideas and views on this topic was interesting. Everyone co-operated and worked well together. It was a lot of fun. The serious topic which the class was dealing with was very thought-provoking. It made us stop and really, really try to remember what happened so long ago – maybe we came out with a better sense of what really happened by telling our own story, but more important how it affected so many people in so many ways.

I am suggesting here two reasons why the arts and arts research are important. First, an aesthetic sensibility allows students to inquire and probe and realize their worlds 'poetically.' To be aestheticized, says Ross (1984), is to be turned toward life, to be attuned to our living process. Second, arts education can drive students to create something about which they can be proud. This is not mere perfectionism, but a profound sense that their work is of value. Cecily O'Neill (1995) describes it as a kind of aesthetic necessity that begins to operate in the group. Pitman's (1998) understanding of this sense of conviction often awakened in teenagers by the arts is fitting:

> This generation has no reason to trust either the ethics or judgement of their elders, but their loyalty to a great idea, a special sound or image, is boundless. It has the potential to save the planet and the human species, but it will also enable them to support themselves and their families.

These two notions – an aesthetic orientation to learning and the pride and confidence aroused by artistic projects – are reason enough to promote the arts and all curricula that have at their core a student-centred and inquiry-based approach.

The day after our Remembrance Day performance, I received two notes from colleagues:

Kathleen,
I wanted to commend you and your class for their very poignant and thought-provoking presentation. Your kids always do a good job instilling a sense of history while at the same time making it relevant to a young girl in 1994 (and to a greying middle-aged man).
A very evocative piece. Well done.
Jim
P.S. Please read this to your class.

The beauty of receiving this letter from the mathematics teacher was that it confirmed for me what I had been suspecting: that drama can get to the core of some fundamentally human questions and that students can and will make things relevant if they have the freedom to do so. The following letter was written to my students from another colleague:

TO: DRAMA STUDENTS WHO PARTICIPATED IN
    REMEMBRANCE DAY MEMORIAL SERVICE
FROM: Mr Layton

Remembrance Day is a sacred time for me, as some of you know from my ramblings in class. Both of my parents are veterans of the Second War, and others of my family also served in the Canadian contingent in Europe.
   The memorial service last week was particularly sensitive and moving. The entire service was prepared and delivered in a most fitting way to enable our community to experience the true spirit of Remembrance Day.
   Without a doubt, the presentation by your group, using music and movement, touched everyone to the core of our beings. I was not the only one to experience tears as you enabled us to enter into the body and soul of those who experienced the tragedy of war. Your professional presentation was worthy of a much larger

audience; we at St Jude's College School are privileged that you did it just for us. You created a 'sacred space' in our day and I'm sure your efforts enabled many of us to remember at the eleventh hour of the eleventh day so that we might keep faith.

'To remember is to end all wars' was the slogan of many a peace march in past years. You have helped us all to remember.

Thank you, Paul Layton

The arts can inform us about the past while allowing us to envision a different future. This classroom experience taught me a great deal about the many kinds of knowledges (cultural, personal, gendered) that students might bring to classroom projects. In this case, time-bound events became the poetic and artistic ingredients of student learning; and the aesthetic sensibility of a group of students extended far beyond their own experience and into the experiences/learning of others in a school community.

Esteemed Canadian director Robert Lepage (1996), in a conversation with playwright Alison McAlpine, described theatre as having a lot to do with 'putting the audience in contact with the gods' (143). Director Peter Brook (1996) describes the artistic creation in theatre as entering the area that lies between the words. Similarly, episodes in teaching, for those of us lucky enough to be working in the arts with children, reveal those precious moments of learning that compel us to look closely at questions of practice to better understand the sheer potential of our work with students.

Girls need more ways to be powerful in schools. My experience as a drama teacher has repeatedly shown me that girls bring their gendered and cultural knowledge to their dramatic creations in a way that allows them to stand proudly, speak wisely, and see differently. Working in role – that is, improvising the story together rather than learning the lines of a script, or process drama – is concerned with forging a production aesthetic during the process and, equally importantly, teaches students about the social constructs that shape their lives while allowing them to shift perspectives and seek truth in opposites –

to alter action, slow down processes, and create meaning collectively. Meaning, as I see it, consists of a broad set of beliefs about what life is like, how it is put together, and how people can conduct themselves within its structures. As a teacher-researcher, I wanted to study my work with girls in order to make a picture of our learning together, and I wanted that picture to be filled with the perceptions and words of the girls themselves. I believed that educational drama was giving them access to more inclusive and more affirming worlds, helping them to gain confidence in social relations at a time when they most need it. To this end, I systematically studied the five drama classes over two school years, videotaping all their work 'in role,' their reflections 'out of role,' and our ongoing discussions about doing drama together. In my final account, it is certainly their voices that are most persuasive.

Expanding the Question of Equity

Over the last half of the century, feminist scholarship has been concerned with the theoretical discourses of representation (or absence thereof) of women through the texts of many cultural and academic fields, of which education is one. Grumet (1988) questioned the absence – in theory, research, and practice – of the commitments, logic, and contradictions that plague female consciousness. Gaskell et al. (1989), in turn, pointed to a rather large body of literature on sex differences that all too often attempts to explain what it is about girls that leads to their lack of achievement, rather than the problems with the institution or the curriculum that may inhibit girls' success. Building on these ideas, my research offers prolonged and extensive observation of drama in a single-sex classroom and challenges many taken-for-granted assumptions about curriculum and gender.

The call for reform by those interested in improving education for girls takes many different forms. Some advocates insist on adding women's voices to what exists, while others call for a 'new' curriculum (Gaskell and Willinsky, 1995). Some believe there are distinct women's ways of knowing (Gilligan, 1982);

others focus on what is taught or even how it is taught (Sarah, Scott, and Spender, 1988). I am proposing a new way to look at education for girls that offers more, rather than fewer, ways to redress the continued evidence of girls' disadvantages in schools.

Recent reports have indicated that boys are falling below the grade in reading and writing, based on standardized test scores of grade 6 students in Ontario. Many have suggested that education is not working well for anybody, a claim that has given rise to the recent standards movement in North America, Europe, Britain, and Australia. Nonetheless, after two decades of research in the United States, there remains a commonly held view that education may be continuing to fail girls to an even greater extent. We still consistently see that girls begin high school with higher test scores in every academic subject, yet graduate from high school scoring 50 points lower than boys on the SAT (Sadker and Sadker, 1994). In 1999, the statistics gathered by the American Institutes for Research on assessment, course-taking patterns, and career choices formed the basis for a text entitled *Gender Gaps: Where Schools Still Fail Our Children*.

Research conducted in Western Canada shows that girls in single-sex secondary classrooms have higher achievement scores than those in co-educational ones, even within the same schools, in the same subject areas, and with the same teachers (Blair and Sandford, 1999). While I am not promoting single-sex education as the best or even necessarily the most empowering education for girls, I would suggest that single-sex education continues to be a viable and important alternative to co-education. But segregation may not be a popular option for liberal or progressive educationalists, with its connotations and indeed its history of privilege and elitism. This 'elitist' reputation often precluded single-sex education from being part of the harmonious, equal-opportunity discourse of the late twentieth century. But it remains clear from the research and literature that secondary co-education is not working very well for girls.

Part of what I would consider the reactionary qualities of liberal education is that the very mechanisms of oppression are at

work in 'equal' education. One of these mechanisms is the criticism of single-sex schools as inappropriate for a modern, pluralistic society. This criticism is based on a spurious notion of tolerance that, in many cases, eliminates contradiction and perpetuates the status quo. This does not mean, however, that a re-visioning of co-education is not needed. The struggle for equality in education must happen on many playing fields; single-sex education simply offers a different configuration in which girls might experience school success.

Girls and Institutions: The Myth of Co-education

The debate on single-sex versus co-educational schooling has a long and tumultuous history, with both sides claiming to have the best interests of girls in mind. It is not my aim to recapitulate this debate or to propose facile solutions. I do, nonetheless, have some thoughts to share as someone who reluctantly (for many of the reasons cited by proponents of co-education and because my own personal experience of co-education had been a good one) accepted a teaching position in a single-sex school. Having taught for ten years in this specialized context, I do not believe that single-sex schooling or even single-sex classrooms will ever solve the problems of inequality, precisely because creating divisions never fully addresses the fundamental question of how we can co-exist as people. But studying closely one single-sex setting has reaffirmed my support of it. It is an alternative worth preserving because these groupings expose additional ways to probe the issue.

While there is growing concern about inequalities in Canadian schools, there is, simultaneously, less consensus about what equality should look like. Perhaps more than their private-school counterparts, public, single-sex schools can provide an alternative with a deeply democratic purpose. Researching in their African context, authors Friedman and Crawford Cousins (1996) insist that relations of power and control are of central significance to any feminist (or democratic) project and by extension to any debate about the relationship between popular

education and gender. A key task for feminists, they assert, is to understand these relations and transform them when they are oppressive. Acknowledging the gendered nature of schools and creating more alternatives to these inscribed social conventions can only lead to a deeper understanding and greater clarity about what gender equality must look and feel like.

Curiously, though, it is the notion of segregation in girls' schools that most disturbs those who view co-education as the pursuit of egalitarian schooling. I am struck by the primary claim of co-education as a more natural, more equal grouping for girls that prepares them for the competition and challenges they will face in the 'real' world. I am struck by this thinking because co-educational schools segregate boys from girls both explicitly and implicitly in their organization and in their operation. Gender discrimination is a fact of life in most co-educational settings. Separating children according to their sex is considered by many teachers to be a routine and easy means of organization. Dividing children into groups of boys and girls is often used by teachers as a controlling device (Skelton, 1993). Schools do not deliberately set out to teach sex differences, but Sara Delamont (1990) argues that schools are more conservative about sex roles than either the home or the wider society. Feminist researchers in education are always in a process of rethinking the institution in order to better serve the interests of girls and women. Girls now have a right to equal and equitable education, but Zimmerman (1988, cited by Spender, 1982, 123) suggests that a mixed-sex education could undermine that right by subordinating the interests of girls to those of boys under the pretence of equality.

Collis (1987), in her excellent study on real and perceived barriers for adolescent females in computer studies in British Columbia, found quantitative and qualitative differences in males' and females' access to computer opportunities in co-educational schools. She also suggests that schools have not reacted when they saw girls limiting their options by erecting barriers marked 'appropriate behaviour – for a girl' and 'not appropriate – for a girl.' In another Canadian study on working-class

females' perspectives on course enrolment in high school, Gaskell and McLaren (1987) found that these girls believed in equal opportunity and wanted to see girls in nontraditional work, but that their conscious, rational, self-preserving calculations made them 'choose' what they saw as best for themselves. Although they said they 'resisted,' they still chose paths that reproduced both gender and class categories.

What has not been the focus of systemic research, claim Sarah, Scott, and Spender (1988) is the level of confidence that learners have when they embark on a task and the expectations they have of themselves. It is plausible, they suggest, that those who approach educational tasks with the expectation that they will do well are more likely to experience success than those who expect to do poorly. They argue that boys are expected to achieve better results than girls and that they fulfil this expectation; boys establish the 'norm' and girls conform:

> When girls and boys are brought together, there is not a merger of two equally balanced groups, but a submersion of one, while the other can remain virtually unchanged. (59)

Proponents of co-education agree that it is generally a better arrangement for socializing boys. But the social aspects of co-education for girls are those that foster female inferiority and dependence (Sarah et al., 1988, 61). This kind of evidence over the last half of the twentieth century has led most leading scholars concerned with issues of gender and education as well as many professional organizations (American Association of University Women Educational Foundation, 1992, 1998; Canadian Teachers' Federation, 1990; Sadker and Sadker, 1994) to continue to engage with these complex and troubling concerns.

Single-Sex Education: Beginning from 'Ourselves'

Dorothy Smith's work in sociology is very instructive for teachers in schools. In her analysis of the ideological structures of women's exclusion, Smith (1987a) states that there is no one uni-

versal subject from whose perspective knowledge can be simply transformed into an objective and universal account. Feminist theoretical writing, despite deep conceptual differences, has been constructively critical because it has continually pointed to the multiplicity of voices present in educational contexts. Despite an inhospitable political and economic climate, critical educators insist that social differences, inequalities, and stratification must be eliminated if there is to be emancipation from social oppression (Cherryholmes 1988). Smith (1987b) suggests further that women have learned to set aside as irrelevant, to deny, or to obliterate their own subjectivity and experience. If, in sociology, as Smith is suggesting, women have learned to work inside a discourse that they did not have a part in making, then the same might be said of curriculum in the schools. In public education, girls are asked to locate themselves inside a canon that has constructed them as 'other,' as object of study rather than subject. It has not asked girls the question: From where you stand, what does this look like? Smith proposes the difficult job of beginning from ourselves:

> It is this essential return to the experience we ourselves have directly in our everyday worlds that has been the distinctive mode of working in the women's movement – the repudiation of the professional, the expert, the already authoritative tones of the discipline; the science, the formal tradition, and the return to the seriously engaged and very difficult enterprise of discovering how to begin from ourselves. (58)

Smith is certainly not the first in education to propose a way of working that begins from the self, but she vehemently insists upon the gendered nature of this self. If Smith is asking how we can make ourselves the subjects of the sociological act of knowing, then in schools we must also begin to see the plot of the story differently. Just as Women's Studies courses in universities began to ask which texts ought to be studied, a curriculum conscious of gender will relocate women in relation to what is studied by making their 'everyday world' the locus of the

curriculum moment. In other words, what must follow the changing discourse and canon is an approach to curriculum that exposes the actual daily social relations among individuals and groups of individuals. Making the everyday world our concern instructs us to look for the 'inner' organization generating the ordinary features of that world (Smith, 1987b, 99).

Smith's feminist research methodology is interested in realizing a sociology for women that is more than an acknowledgment of a particular standpoint or perspective. It does not universalize a particular experience. It is, rather, 'a method that from the outset of inquiry, creates a space for an absent subject, and absent experience to be filled with the presence and spoken experience of actual women speaking of and in the actualities of their everyday worlds' (107). This description of one kind of feminist research became a strong guideline for my own reflective-teacher research because it insists upon the multiplicity of voices in the research act, voices that articulate the actualities of our daily lives in the classroom. This kind of intimate relationship of research to practice, which is a hallmark of teacher research, is more akin to traditions of feminist and postmodern methodologies than to academic traditions of technical rationality.

Like Smith, Kazemeck (1995), in her work on reading and female moral development, insists that a multi-perspective view of life recognizes the importance of the imagination. The imagination, she concludes, is seen as creative, transformative, and potentially subversive because it allows us to construct alternatives to dominant perceptions and ways of being in the world. Grugeon (1993), in her study of the gender implications of children's playground culture, discovered that the clapping games that girls play in the schoolyard are essentially cooperative, rule-governed, and ritualistic, not hierarchical or competitive, and that they actually enable girls to manipulate language, rehearse adult roles, and investigate and challenge the social and sexual aspects of the world as they become involved in peer-group relations.

Daley (1991) reported on an extensive national American survey on gender and self-esteem in which 3000 boys and girls

were polled on attitudes toward self, school, family, and friends. For girls, the passage into adolescence is marked by a loss of confidence in themselves and their abilities, a developing critical attitude toward their bodies, along with a growing sense of personal inadequacy. Many more studies that chart the rather rapid decline of self-worth experienced by girls in our public school systems might also be named. Suffice it to say that gender blindness does not equal gender equity. Knowing this, I began to think about how to deliver more honestly the promise of equality in education. The impetus behind my teacher research, then, was to recast the relationship between girls and classrooms by asking the girls themselves to describe their experiences of a curriculum as they worked with/through the conventions of drama in education.

In short, researchers make a great many hypotheses in their studies on single-sex learning in schools. For instance, it is often suggested that girls experience fear of success and that such fears may be overcome in a single-sex setting if educators value the achievements of women, transmit high expectations to them, and foster more androgynous definitions of self. This would ensure that being female is not viewed as inconsistent with achievement (Monaco and Gaier, 1992). In Draper's (1993) study on the re-establishment of gender relations following a school merger of two single-sex schools (one girls' school and one boys' school) with one co-educational school, she found that in science the girls did not take advantage of their prior progress to remain ahead of the boys, but responded to the masculine signals they were receiving and permitted the boys to dominate the lesson. Lockheed and Hall's (cited by Monaco and Gaier 1992) conclusions in their work on groups and leadership patterns indicate that, in general, men play competitively with a strong motive to win while women attempt to achieve the best for all players. They form alliances to minimize both their own losses as well as those of others. Furthermore, the findings suggest that women are unlikely to emerge as group leaders in mixed-sex groups regardless of leadership style or dominance level. I would suggest that rather than offer courses on 'women' in an attempt to

raise women's achievement behaviours (which seems to be the preferred response to the self-perception problem of girls in mixed-sex schools), single-sex schools should simply provide more leadership experiences and allow girls to define themselves according to the greater expectations placed on them.

Dale Spender (1982), in her influential work *Invisible Women – The Schooling Scandal*, makes a strong case for single-sex education, stating that 'while the web of male influence extends and expands, however, female influence appears to be negligible in the presence of males, for female students stand in subordination both to teachers and to their male classmates, in most conventional classrooms' (118). Her argument is convincing in that it explores what single-sex schools are *not* doing rather than what they *are* doing. In exposing the harmful effects of mixed-sex education, she advocates single-sex education for its lack of potentially damaging experiences for girls. In looking closely at power structures in the classroom, and in challenging the familiar accusation that single-sex schools are 'unreal' or 'artificial,' Spender admits that they are, in fact, artificial in that they do not provide girls with a group to whom they are required to defer, nor boys with a group whom they can dominate. Boys, she finds, do not perform as well when they have no one to dominate, or when there is no 'inferior' group against which to measure themselves.

Single-sex schooling for girls, as a temporary grouping during the trying years of adolescence, offers some noteworthy benefits for girls. Separatism is not a goal in itself, but education should make a person more powerful, competent, and capable. For female students, says Lips (1987), an increased sense of their own power might begin with an educational system on which they feel able to have an impact. Experiencing power within a system might well lead to confidence that stretches beyond the boundaries of that system. Single-sex schools, in my view, merely begin to interrupt the cycle of oppression and allow girls the much-needed space to rearticulate the multiplicitous construction of the 'self' before taking on the larger and more dichotomous nature of gender relations. It is a space that can

take the reality of heterogeneity seriously. But these schools, too, must explicitly engage questions of gender, race, and class inequalities if they are to be sites of emancipatory education and offer a way to re-imagine how knowledge is produced, shared, and built upon.

Three weeks before my doctoral defence in 1998, I was listening to a CBC (Canadian Broadcasting Corporation) radio interview with the principal researcher of the American Association of University Women's 1998 report on single-sex schooling. It was suggested that their 1998 findings negated their 1992 research that had found single-sex schooling generally better for girls. Their current findings, the interviewer reported, implied that although girls feel better in single-sex schools and believe they are doing better, there was, in fact, no evidence of this. My first thoughts were: How can this be? Girls feel better but aren't doing better? I wondered what they meant by 'success.' Academic success? Success in sciences and maths? How was this success measured? My second thought, of course, was that my entire dissertation committee was also listening to CBC radio that evening and my case for single-sex education had just collapsed. I immediately ordered the report from Washington and was surprised and affirmed by reading it. In fact (and what was not reported in the interview), girls who are traditionally or historically less privileged (by race/ethnicity, class) are the ones who stand to gain the most from single-sex education. These smaller single-sex schools in the United States – often Catholic and serving less privileged populations – provide the most opportunities for girls' success. I felt reaffirmed in my case for single-sex education for girls as a viable alternative that can address questions of equity and multiculturalism in innovative ways.

It is in doing drama with girls where I have discovered the most powerful examples of emancipatory education. In drama, we can begin nowhere else but from 'ourselves,' where the personal and the cultural have a place. It is important then to provide here a description of the context in which we found ourselves 'doing drama.'

Our Setting

Context affects learning. Each school and each classroom within a school has unique features that distinguish it from all other environments. Some of the individual characteristics of the school where I conducted my research are worth describing in some detail. This is not meant to preclude generalizations but, rather, to illustrate the process of reflexivity and analysis at the heart of teacher research. The school's urban mix of race and ethnicity, socioeconomic class, academic ability, along with its Catholic ethos, are important in understanding the context in which these girls relate to each other. It is in the specificity of qualitative research findings where the greatest perceptions lie.

St Jude's was founded in 1854 and was originally conceived as a place for traditional academic, Catholic education for young ladies, servicing a rather homogeneous and socioeconomically privileged population. Anecdotal evidence suggests that the segregation of boys and girls at that time was meant to benefit the boys by removing the 'distraction' of girls. The Sisters who founded the school taught a traditional English, science, and maths curriculum; well-turned-out ladies made better prospects for marriage or for convent life. The girls were largely from Anglo-Saxon, English-speaking, privileged backgrounds. The girls' marks and rankings were read aloud before all the parishioners at Sunday mass. In other words, the performance of the girls was subjected to the judgment and scrutiny of the community and measured according to its 'norms.' It was a very parochial and hierarchical system, noted for its 'academic [white, middle-class] excellence.' The staff, originally made up of nuns and priests, now consists of lay women and men and has no teachers from the religious order. Much has changed in the school today, but this history, together with the greatly changed student and staff population of the formerly private and now publicly funded institution, makes it a unique site for the education of young women.

The school, originally built for 600 students, now has over 1,200 students and might be described as an inner-city school. Of

its population, 29.9 per cent were not born in Canada and 65.7 per cent do not speak English as a first language (Spanish and Portuguese are the dominant 'home' languages). There is also a much more significant representation of working-class and refugee families, although there remains a much smaller population of girls from middle-class families. Within the school, forty-four different nationalities are represented.

The student timetables suggest that the school still has an English, science, and math focus. The school hosts debating tournaments and is heavily involved in science fairs and University of Waterloo math contests. Although the arts are called upon regularly to 'represent' the school (particularly at public-relations events, school assemblies, and in the interpretation of the gospel at school liturgies), the real thrust of the school seems to be in the area of sciences, following a more traditional, academic model of schooling.

It would seem that the administration and the staff of the school are interested in retaining a certain 'excellence' – that is, an academic focus – in spite of the less homogeneous population of the school. Within its district of schools, St Jude's has retained its reputation as a serious academic school, but has clearly modified its curriculum to accommodate academically challenged and non–English-speaking students by adding a rapidly growing number of 'special education' and 'English as a second language' courses. Despite being a publicly funded school, however, there remain signs of its private-school heritage, such as the uniforms the girls wear.

St Jude's also emphasizes the importance of the school 'community,' which gathers frequently throughout the school year to celebrate masses and religious holidays. There is also a population of non-Catholics in the school. Nevertheless, St Jude's, in its 'public' incarnation, has maintained its Catholic ethos. All students must study religion each year, which leaves fewer options in their programs of study for such courses as drama, music, art, languages, and physical education. The school has a strong sports program, although this is an extracurricular focus, rather than a curricular pursuit. The more traditional academic lean-

ings of the school suggest that it has attempted to retain the traditional educational pursuits of 'excellence' while embracing the reality of the more heterogeneous population it serves.

The students at St Jude's come from approximately forty different 'feeder' (elementary) schools, located in a number of neighbourhoods in the Toronto area. Therefore, the educational backgrounds of the incoming students vary considerably. The school has exceptionally identified students (both 'gifted' and academically challenged streams, with particular programs for both) as well as general-level (applied) and advanced-level (academic) streams. The dramatic arts curriculum has always been offered at the advanced level only, but is available to all students in the school as an arts option, regardless of their academic stream of study.

In the new Ontario Ministry of Education (2000) designations, arts programs in schools will be 'open' (rather than academic or applied), which will again result in the most heterogeneous groupings possible. Each class, therefore, has a range from the brightest to the weakest (academically) and no attempt is made to 'stream' the students who opt for drama. Dramatic arts, music, religion, and physical education are the only areas in which this kind of destreamed mix would occur. In a typical grade 10 drama class, at the time of my research, about 35 per cent of the group would be from the advanced-level stream, 32 per cent from the general-level stream, 25 per cent would be identified with learning disabilities, and the remaining 8 per cent would be labelled as 'gifted.' In each class there were seven to twelve 'new Canadians' – those students who have been working in an 'English as a second language' stream for five years or less. Grade 10 students are usually 14 or 15 years old, although much older students often come to the class who are studying drama for the first time.

In a traditional single-sex school such as this one, the drama class represents a more relaxed atmosphere to the students. There are no chairs or desks; there are plants and fish, and articles on bulletin boards about arts events in the city. The students sit in a circle, on carpets on the floor. The room, whose walls are

bedecked with colourful posters of student seminar work, has a less 'institutional' look than the rest of the school. Clearly, the environment in the drama class is more conducive to informal discussion and freer movement about the room. It is a much less structured place, and the students and teacher share the space in a less formal or hierarchical way than they do in other classrooms.

It is critical for a teacher to study her or his own context. The classroom is the field where we labour, and knowing that domain in all its particularities helps us to see the limits and possibilities for growth. It is onto this background that I have set the girls' perceptions and insights. I offer a window onto our world, a picture of girls' stories – the detailed reflections of a teacher-researcher and her students and our experiences together in a drama classroom.

Chapter Two

Creators of Worlds

Drawing was no more than copying, and I didn't care for art, all the more so because I was not very good at it: I reacted to the general appearance of an object without paying much attention to its details; I could never succeed in drawing even the simplest flower. In compensation, I knew how to use language and as it expressed the essence of things, it illuminated them for me. I had a spontaneous urge to turn everything that happened to me into a story: I used to talk freely, and loved to write. If I was describing in words an episode in my life, I felt that it was being rescued from oblivion, that it would interest others, and so be saved from extinction. I loved to make up stories, too: when they were inspired by my own experience, they seemed to justify it; in one sense they were of no use at all, but they were unique and irreplaceable, they existed, and I was proud of having snatched them out of nothingness.

Simone de Beauvoir, *Memoirs of a Dutiful Daughter* (1959)

Living through Stories

Together, we snatched our stories out of nothingness and saved them from extinction. There is, I think, something of a Simone de Beauvoir in all young women. Doing drama and building stories creates a restlessness and a tension in the room; it is about ascertaining the imperatives of the group. The social intercourse in drama is about more than being sensitive to others; it is about being sensitized by the actions and words of others. My endless hours of videotaped lessons of our drama activities together revealed four distinct areas of learning and helped me to under-

stand and frame the different kinds of learning drama can initiate. I have named these four emergent areas: Drama and Expressive Learning; Drama and Intelligence; Drama as Collective Process; and Drama as Personal Development.

In this chapter, I have included excerpts of classroom discussions about our drama in and out of role for each of these areas of learning. I have also described, in some detail, the sources and theatre conventions used in order that the references to classroom work and students' insights can be placed within these created contexts. The subsequent references to their writing and reflections can then be understood within the framework of the collectively created worlds of the dramas.

For each of the dramas I describe, it is important to understand that the sources used are not playscripts but stories, picture books, folk tales, and magazine articles, which provide the initial imperative for exploration. Drama teachers have the difficult but exciting task of selecting material that they believe will interest their students. Because they are not following a textbook, they have the whole of the history of life and literature to choose from, along with the many powerful symbols of popular culture to draw on. Freire often spoke to teachers about what he referred to as 'prepackaged teacher education.' He resisted the use of teacher-proof materials, suggesting that these were a sign of a lack of faith on the part of 'experts' in the possibility that teachers can know and can also create. Knowing one's own context intimately is the first step in realizing a curriculum for learning. For teachers beginning to use drama in the classroom, it might be useful to think of these sources or generators of curriculum as the trigger or springboard for improvised exploration. My own methodology is similar to that of others who work in an improvised mode for learning. A context is created, usually originating from a story source that introduces the kind of world we are in and the sorts of tensions characters in that world might be encountering.

From my classroom teaching, I have found that adolescents are often grappling with representations of authority and with conflicts that address the difficult questions of 'right and

wrong,' 'truth and fiction,' 'poverty and wealth,' 'self and other.' The 'social issues' of some urgency to adolescents often include questions of 'freedom,' 'oppression,' and 'relationships.' They are also drawn to situations that ask them to explore their identity and individuality. As a teacher, I am looking for sources that provide some context for investigation of these complex concerns. I also use a 'what happens when' approach to our story-making rather than a 'what happens next' approach, which often invites the stronger, more confident voices to control the collective creating. As facilitator of the drama, I am aiming to set up a structure that may evoke many different directions. Once we have explored what might have happened, we can ask again 'Now what happens when ...' and change the details or invite new voices into the story-making. This gets us away from the 'what's next' approach, a more sequential or linear construction. The following drama examples will employ this 'what happens when' stance that I prefer.

For each of the categories of learning, I shall describe the sources I selected that I hoped would be engaging to 15-year-old girls. Once into the stories, as teacher I drew on specific conventions, that I will describe in detail, to propel us through these emerging worlds. It is always the aim of the drama teacher to challenge students to move beyond superficial and often stereotypical depictions of life and to assist them in exploring all the dimensions of their improvised characters and worlds. Table 2.1 indicates the dramatic structures used and the characteristics of the four categories of learning observed in the process dramas.

Drama and Expressive Learning

'Mary Morgan'

Artistic expression as a significant and persistent category in student work became especially evident as I studied their aesthetic choices of form within representations of dramatic worlds. This category, as well, provided the most evidence of affective learning among the students. Broadly stated, students rehearsed

Table 2.1

Type of Learning: **Drama and Expressive Learning**
Source/Pretext: 'Mary Morgan'
Dramatic Convention: 'A Day in the Life,' 'Letter Writing'
Observations:
- Personal engagement with images
- Manipulating form in aesthetic presentation
- Constructing perspectives
- Context and form working together

Type of Learning: **Drama and Intelligence**
Source/Pretext: 'Kelly Turner,' 'Philip Malloy'
Dramatic Convention: 'Still Images,' 'Forum Theatre,' 'Hot Seating'
Observations:
- Learning through spontaneous engagement in the activity
- Cognitive functions to accommodate alternative perspectives and ideas
- Changed consciousness in fictional world as indicator of cognitive development
- Engagement of values/belief systems
- Inviting tension and contradiction

Type of Learning: **Drama as Collective Process**
Source/Pretext: 'Maudie-Ann,' 'Kerry Smith'
Dramatic Convention: 'Forum Theatre,' 'Writing in Role,' 'Interviewing'
Observations:
- Collective negotiation of meaning
- Participant-actors and participant-audience in context building
- 'Final product' as collage of ideas and images
- Challenge to move beyond stereotype in character delineation

Type of Learning: **Drama as Personal Development**
Source/Pretext: 'Earthwoman'
Dramatic Convention: 'Forum Theatre,' 'Meeting,' 'Letter Writing,' 'Ceremonies,' 'Writing in Role'
Observations:
- Fictional world as mediator between actual lives of students and fictional lives of characters
- Students determine what they need to learn
- Group – story closure as provisional
- Students and authorship

---

and replayed choices of movement, dialogue, and music to further explore the life of a character at a critical moment.

The source used as our starting point was the story of 'Mary Morgan' in which Green (1990) recalls the life of a poor servant girl, impregnated by the son of the squire of the house where she

is employed. In her efforts to conceal the pregnancy, she kills her baby at birth. The details in this short synopsis are the only ones the students knew when they began their exploration. The story evoked strong feelings in the students – some sympathized, some judged, some condemned – but they all wanted to understand the actions of the character.

After this initial introduction, we spent little time retelling the story or replaying the events, but used the 'what happens when' approach to flesh out the context and the people of the story. The students soon became keenly interested in the complexities of the character. What happens when someone of her age, of her education, of her circumstances, finds herself in this situation? The students began trying on different 'selves' or masks in response to the ambiguities and the contradictions they felt. Over time, positions were clarified in the room because of the tensions of differing opinions, and students understood these positions as collectively shaped. Their choices were always made in view of the others' positions. Gavin Bolton (1971) argues that when drama is a group sharing of a dramatic situation, it is more powerful than any other medium in education. The students became acutely aware of the complexities of the story, whether they were playing Mary herself or another character they imagined into the work.

Dramatic Structures I

Dramatic or theatrical structures are conventions used by drama teachers to 'get inside' the characters and dilemmas of drama sources. In this first illustration, the structures served to engage the emotions of the students. 'It felt sad to portray Mary Morgan because we felt her hurt, sadness, and loneliness,' reflected one student. I instructed the class, in their groups, to use the convention of 'a day in the life' to develop their ideas about the central character. Their affective learning became most apparent in their presentations of 'A Day in the Life' of Mary Morgan, a structure that uses the world of theatre to deepen understanding of a dramatic world. 'A day in the life' is a dramatic structure described

by Neelands (1990, 27) as 'a convention [that] works backwards from an important event in order to fill in the gaps in the history of how the characters have arrived at the event.' In this way, a chronological sequence was built up from the scenes prepared by two groups (the class divided in half) that involved the central character, Mary Morgan, at different times in the preceding twenty-four hours before she killed her child.

After a brief mapping out and rehearsal of their scenes, each group had the opportunity to see the dramatic presentation of the other group and subsequently redraft their own scenes to take into account the influence of the other group's interpretation. What they created in the end was a series of short vignettes that attempted to represent the emotions and thoughts of this character at this particular moment in her life. Barton and Booth (1990) describe the use of structures of this kind as a meaning-making endeavour that interprets life and helps us to understand our world. In this way, they say, it is like other art forms in that it uses symbols as a means of shaping and crafting and expressing feelings and ideas while participants are involved both as spectator and participant in exploration and in performance. In other words, students learned about theatrical and aesthetic presentation by manipulating form and controlling the medium. 'Symbols signify various things at the same time, and many things to different people,' says Courtney (1989, 206) in describing the multi-vocal quality of dramatic symbols. One student, referring specifically to her group's crafting of the character's dilemma, explained: 'I felt that we could create our own aspect of her life.' Another claimed, 'It was fun to act in someone else's life, that we were able to do what we want.'

Four particular students, in their reflections after the drama work, summarized best the potential for expressive learning through personal engagement with images. One student admitted, 'I felt that I was actually a part of the storyline and that I was a part of Mary Morgan's life.' Another offered, 'I didn't really feel as bad as she must have felt. But when we did it in class, I could kinda see what she was going through.' The next two classmates, referring to the specific dramatic structure used, expressed a somewhat more sophisticated understanding of dramatic pre-

sentation as a means of exploring both content and form: 'A Day in the Life of Mary Morgan scared me. I felt like it was actually happening. Performing scenes helps to realize exactly what was happening and how each character felt.' Barton and Booth (1990) suggest that drama in schools and youth theatres only occurs when students experience the content and form together as one and when the art of theatre is felt and understood within the context of the work being explored. Ruby reflects:

> Playing a day in the life of Mary Morgan (like all drama presentations) required quite a bit of imagination and interpretation of who I feel a certain character is. In a sense it requires finding a certain quality of a particular character within yourself and improvising on that.

Some students seemed to make further extensions of their learning into their lives and the real world they experience beyond their created world. The social metaphor explored in the re-creation of Mary's day was a representation of actions associated with actual experience, in this case an historical account of the life of a servant girl. Neelands (1990) suggests:

> The purpose of metaphor in theatre, as in other art-forms, is to invite comparison between what is being symbolically represented and the real area of experience that is referred to. Part of the learning experience of theatre is in recognizing and constructing connections between the fiction of the drama and the real events and experiences the fictions draw on. As the theatrical activity unfolds, the fictional situation and characters become more and more recognizable to the creators of the drama, and the relationships begin to form between what is happening in the drama and what happens in the outside world. (69)

Gisella, making a forward leap, as Courtney (1986) would say, returns to this 'outside world' in her explanation:

> It made me feel lucky along with happy that I didn't live in Mary Morgan's time and that women have come a long way and have

gone through a lot to get to where I am now and it also makes me
feel hopeful for the future of women in today's society.

Expressive learning often provides unanticipated learning
opportunities for students. In this particular drama, many students struggled with the question of the 'truth' of a situation in
their post-drama written reflections. What seemed to happen
increasingly in their role-playing was a decreasing concern with
knowing what 'really happened' and a growing consciousness
of the fact that they were 'constructing' the truth, which several
called 'many-sided' or changeable. Rosa expressed it this way:

> I learned that in every situation everyone views their own story as
> the truth, builds up their own truth. And through acting out dif-
> ferent points of view we understood why everyone wanted their
> story to be the truth.

Rather than empathy for a 'point of view,' Rosa is expressing the
feeling that she understands why someone might need to
believe her own creation of the truth. This, it would seem, is
beyond an appreciation of the 'other.' It is perhaps closer to an
understanding of how we are all players with vested interests,
inventing our personalities and constructing our social worlds.

Finally, beyond their reflections out of role, there was also evidence of expressive learning in role, in their writing. In this case,
I used the exercise of 'Letter Writing' with the students to 'build
up a cumulative account of a long sequence of work' (Neelands,
1990, 17). The following letter excerpt demonstrates the students' ability to provide an imagined audience and adopt an
appropriate register and vocabulary to deepen the understanding of the role-playing work:

> Dear Wilki,
> I'm in jail now replaying my life over and over again. Thinking of
> all that has happened to get me here. As I think back I remember
> what a huge role you played in my life ... We did what we could
> but it just didn't work. As much as I regret doing what we did, I
> realize in the times in which we live, we had no choice. But I still

hate myself for it. I just keep thinking how could I steal someone else's life when I too was robbed of mine ... Maybe we will be reunited in another life where love is the only thing that matters and money and status don't.

Love, Mary

This letter was written collectively by six students in the class. They then took their letter and made choices of form in a theatre mode in order to theatrically and symbolically express their understanding of the situation they were conveying. The students were, therefore, asked to demonstrate skills and knowledge relating to the art form, since they were required to choose theatrical conventions, gesture, and movement appropriate to their created context.

These examples of the 'Mary Morgan' drama created moments in which the students understood that content and form worked together. Their expressive learning within a contextualized drama was easily observable. They were able to structure action and to work within specific theatre conventions while developing theatre vocabulary and performance skills. Most apparent in their reflections was a gaining of insight and understanding of the characters and the events as a direct result of their engagement with the theatrical convention. What I have called 'expressive learning' here emerged from what might be best understood as the articulation and resolution of emotional conflicts and tensions in our improvised story. It is this quality of interaction among students often witnessed by drama teachers that suggests the important role drama will play in the development and exercising of communication skills. Negotiating in role enhances the students' opportunities for understanding the qualities of successful relationships.

Drama and Intelligence

'Kelly Turner'

At a time when 'standards' and testing are touted as the remedies for all that ails schools, it is not surprising to anyone work-

ing in the arts that the opportunities to integrate the arts across the curriculum are being diminished. However, there is a body of evidence, which arts organizations and commissions on learning have continually referenced, that illustrates the intellectual advantages afforded students of the arts. Pitman (1998) convincingly argues that all the arts – music, drama, dance, the visual and technological arts – should be integrated into the instructional process in every discipline:

> The quality of life for future generations depends on how this debate about learning resolves itself in Canada. A very important aspect of this debate will be the degree to which the arts, individually as disciplines and integrated in their full power, will be recognized as essential and as pathways to intellectual mastery and emotional stability in an uncertain age. (88)

For our next drama, the classes began to explore the story of 'Kelly Turner' with a simple photocopied picture, taken from a magazine article about a 15-year-old girl. This girl was to become the protagonist of their created world. I was introduced to this source myself in a drama workshop at Toronto's Young People's Theatre, facilitated by Jonathon Neelands and Warwick Dobson. Spontaneous role-playing conventions were used in this drama as a means of deepening and layering the character to suggest her complexities. In the classes, therefore, choices of content illustrated a cognitive and, in some cases, moral development among students. Through their work, the students articulated questions of 'right and wrong,' of values, beliefs, and cultural understanding.

Spontaneous Role-Playing and Cognition

Parts of the magazine story of 'Kelly Turner' were shared with the students, as a pretext (O'Neill, 1995) or springboard into the dramatic activity. The article describes a 15-year-old girl who learns from her boyfriend of a violent, racial attack on a Southeast Asian boy in which he and his friends were involved. She is

torn about reporting what she knows. Process drama often begins with such a dilemma: a choice to be made, a decision to take, a side to stand on. Students began to consider questions about the 'relations of ruling' or the social constructs operating in the lives of the characters. Smith's (1987b, 188) idea is that seeing the 'everyday world as problematic' is seeing that social relations external to it are present in its organization.

My task began with pulling different perspectives into focus by employing conventions that freeze a problem in time in order to explore it from several vantage points. Acting something like a sociologist, I again used drama conventions to help students shift the lens through which they were focusing in order to see the dilemma from a variety of perspectives. In this way, they began to see plainly the ways in which our 'perspective' is shaped by the social constructs organizing that perspective. Once again, as we saw in the story of 'Mary Morgan,' this lesson, too, affords students the possibility of living, however briefly, inside the walls of the dilemma: should our heroine tell what she knows and risk her own and her family's safety? The written-reflection aspect of the lesson afforded students the possibility of standing outside the dilemma and asking questions.

First, I asked the students to take an excerpt from the article and find a physical representation for the events described in the excerpt. I impressed upon them that it was not the violence we were interested in conveying but the thoughts and feelings that might be present in such a violent scene. The following graphic excerpt is the initial source the students were given to work with:

The near-fatal attack happened in Bethnal Green after the Valentine's Day disco last February. Around 20 white teenage boys chased a Bengali student down a side street and set on him in a frenzy of racial hatred. Kicking his head like a football until his scalp became detached from his skull, the gang left their 18-year-old victim, Mukhta Ahmed, in a two-day coma, with facial injuries so severe that he was unrecognizable.

They only stopped kicking him when a woman living in the flats

nearby came out and shouted at them. They ran off and she cradled Mukhta in her arms and talked to him until the police came.

I asked the students to try to capture the feeling of the scene, instructing that the only necessary words/sounds should be the reaction of the woman when she shouted to the gang (What might she shout? How might she sound?), and, finally, that they should end their scene, as the article explains, with the woman comforting the boy. When the four groups in the class were ready to share these scenes, they did so in a kind of 'theatre in the round,' occupying space all around the room, with the end of one group's work signalling the beginning of the next group, and so on until all four scenes were complete. This allows for a kind of spontaneous and collective representation and gets students away from the comparing and competing that often create an unhelpful kind of self-consciousness during this kind of exploratory work. With this initial scene creation, the students aimed to capture the horror of the crime.

Next, I asked the students to create 'still images' representing 'illustrations' of key events. These images were then used to freeze the frame or hold the action in order for the students to reflect on the images and collect their questions. Groups of approximately six students were asked to use their bodies to physically devise an image that crystallized a moment in Kelly's life. Neelands (1990, 19) describes this convention as a highly selective way of forming meaning into concrete images, which is a very economical and controlled form of expression, as well as a sign to be interpreted or read by observers. This convention often communicates more than words alone can. A manipulation of time – freezing moments, as it were – is often used by drama teachers to allow students time to digest ideas and possibly recommend changes. Theoretically, this means that there is time to hear the thinking in the room so that positions are shaped collectively as ideas are sharpened against each other. These images are then brought to life when the teacher – also in role – enters the image. With a sense of risk, we began improvising together the conversations the characters might be having.

This is where I easily recognized the spontaneity and intelligence of these students.

In this exercise, these re-created contexts in the protagonist's life were not scenes the students already knew, but scenes they might imagine. In other words, it is not simply about what you know, it is about using what you know to imagine. Schools would do well to call on this kind of independent and creative thinking much more. I, as 'teacher-in-role,' moved into these various contexts, calling on the students to improvise the action spontaneously. Moving a character through different social contexts illustrates facets of that character and key moments in a life. Learning through drama happens through engagement in the activity, and not, as is often suggested, through perfecting a performance technique, or 'lying' convincingly. The students discovered that people behave very differently in different contexts and that their own thinking about the dilemma is largely shaped by the 'roles' they take on. Siobhan reflected:

When we were role-playing as the different people in Kelly's life, I played the role of Kelly's father. At first it was difficult as I assumed that the beliefs of Kelly's father were different from my own. This difficulty disappeared once I got a sense of this character and what he would have been feeling and I came to view the situation from a new perspective. I continued to believe that the right thing for her to do was to go to the police with her information, but I began to understand how a person could feel differently. His beliefs became my beliefs when I was in role and this gave me a good perspective from which to attack this role. In a role such as this, I found that it was essential not to break character as it is sometimes difficult to find that character again once it has been lost. I also found that when performing the role of a character you become that character. It is as if you are no longer yourself and yet you are; but you are completely taken over by this alternate identity.

Students draw on cognitive functions in order to accommodate 'other perspectives' and alternative ideas. Courtney's

(1990) investigations of drama's role in intellectual development addressed questions of the nature of human intelligence and cognition, making particular reference to the acting mode of 'as if' in spontaneous drama. He suggested that intelligence means more than a person's capacity to function well or badly in the world with people, information, and environments. It is, rather, those cognitive skills valued in a specific culture. Gardner (1983), in his theory of multiple intelligences, argued that intelligence is not a static, measurable entity, but also includes linguistic, logical-mathematical, bodily-kinesthetic, spatial, musical, and personal intelligences. Cognition is often used to describe the activities of the mind that process information, but cognition as understood in the drama class is better described as mental concepts that become the basis for ideas and the dynamics between ideas. Therefore, cognition in the drama classroom can be understood as information processing and concept formation, as in Courtney's (1990) theory of 'dramatic intelligence':

> Our creative imagination and dramatic actions are experienced as a whole, and together they create meaning. They bring about the 'as if' world of possibility (the fictional), which works in parallel with the actual world and is a cognitive tool for understanding it. (9)

Delanie reflected on her experience of the 'as if' or 'dramatic knowing' in a situation after her experience of spontaneous role-play:

> Before I role-played as Kelly's sister, I didn't really see the significance of Kelly's situation. To me it was like, 'just tell the police and get it over with.' I learned I was wrong though. There is much more to it than that. As I role-played, I could really feel the conflicts involved in the situation. The family was scared of what might happen to them. Even though this was a main concern, they trusted her in deciding the right thing for her to do. It made me change the way I felt about her situation by realizing that her decision affects not only her life but the lives of others as well.

It was also clear in group discussions in the classroom and in written reflections that students began to think about people as social beings, related to each other in significant ways. It became obvious that their thinking about Kelly's dilemma broadened as they filled out the context of Kelly's life, shifted the lens through which they were looking, and considered many of the social aspects of her life. Students are often keen to discuss ideas together during this kind of improvised work. In one such discussion, Carla remarked on her evolution in thinking:

> When I was role-playing, I knew that I was no longer viewing the situation as a spectator, but a family member who is affected by Kelly's decision. As Kelly's family we had a strong influence on her. This made it tough because every word and action we did could have triggered her to react differently.

Lizzie, role-playing as Kelly's friend, also began to see the connectedness of people as she explained:

> When I was role-playing as Kelly's friend it made me question my original thought of cooperating with the police. It made me realize how truly difficult it would be to advise someone in that predicament. I felt that if I leaned to one way, it might affect Kelly's decision, which then might turn out to be the wrong decision. I felt confused and with mixed feelings. I knew what was right and wrong in my opinion, but I basically felt that I should just be supportive.

In another role-playing exercise, Ashley's initial ideas were supported and confirmed by the role-playing her group engaged in. This required them to jump backward and forward in their thinking as details filled in the picture, resulting in a continuous assessment of their own thinking:

> When we role-played we showed the situation as very violent as it probably was when it happened. When playing the bully it

really made me feel even more strongly about my decision 'I would tell' if I was in that situation.

What I could hear in my students' reflections on their improvised theatrical creations was the intellectual considerations a playwright might engage in while creating a plot and characters. Using this contextualized and improvised theatrical device, the students were simultaneously scripting and interpreting their own ideas.

Change as a Significant Indicator of Cognitive Development

I would like to consider elements of role-play during our work with the 'Kelly Turner' drama that resulted, for several students, in an experience of changed consciousness. Improvisation and other forms of dramatic expression were used to move the fictional action forward. What became clear was that students, whose understanding of a dramatic world that is based on their experience of an actual world and their personal criteria for making judgments, can be poignantly challenged by dramatic role-play. Courtney (1990) offers that the actual world uses enactment for externalizing imaginings in many media, while our dramatic world uses enactment to test our knowing of actuality.

Change, then, can take place in the creative imagination. If, as Courtney (1990) argues, the 'as if' is the way we understand life and existence, then the player may experience the dramatic world as an alternative to the actual world but one that, beyond metaphor, is related to and can influence the actual world. In short, the fictional, while presenting a particular view of truth, also challenges previous understandings of 'the truth' of a situation. It is these new possibilities for students that engage them in the mental work of role-play in drama.

The following reflections of students highlight their reformulation of concepts based on their role-playing experiences in class. It is startling to note the number of students who rely on the metaphor of 'being in another's shoes' to explain their changed perceptions. The playwright Tom Stoppard (1995) once

defined his art as a means of contradicting oneself in public. For Luisa, the changes seemed to be more than mere contradiction:

> The role-playing of police ... changed me because it was like putting myself in other people's shoes. I realized this because I thought of her situation and how hard it would be to make the right decision without affecting or hurting close family members and friends.

Bianca also attributed her deepened understanding to the role-playing exercise and suggested the possibility for embodied knowledge in dramatic role-play:

> When I was role-playing as Kelly's teacher, it changed the way that I was looking at the situation quite a bit, because when I was actually *in the teacher's shoes*, I tended to think differently than I would have if I just *thought* of what the teacher would have done.

Alex, also in the role of Kelly's teacher, articulated precisely how ideas are challenged in role and how new questions previously unknown or unconsidered become relevant:

> When I role-played as Kelly's teacher, it changed the way I was looking at the situation because now I was looking through someone else's eyes. Since we started this 'Kelly Turner' story, we were always asking the question 'How would Kelly feel?' When I role-played as her teacher I asked the question 'How do I feel about this situation?' Looking from someone else's point of view changed your whole outlook on the situation because you begin to realize everything and everyone was a factor in Kelly's decision.

Drama and Moral Development

Not surprisingly, the 'Kelly Turner' drama gave rise to much discussion about 'right and wrong' among the students in their post-drama reflections. The few cited below demonstrate understandings that attempted to take account of personal and

cultural differences in moral development. In the case of 'Kelly Turner,' the actions of the drama made the students' thoughts social – that is, they introduced into the social sphere their values and belief systems. Jennifer summarized it in this way:

> Right and wrong has to be decided by the individual. Kelly's story showed me that big problems aren't out in a neat pattern; it isn't just black and white. Yet, in the end, right and wrong comes down to moral opinions and values which are learned, not felt from the beginning of life.

For Melissa, a visible-minority student, the lessons were less complicated:

> It taught me about both right and wrong. The fact that those gangsters were beating up an oriental guy just because of his race seemed very wrong. The story also taught me about right when Kelly Turner told the cops about what she knew.

Tenisha offered the following explanation about 'right and wrong' based on her experiences in the group role-playing:

> Kelly Turner's story taught me that everyone knows right from wrong, although at times they may [be] hard to distinguish. Your conscience helps you follow your morals and to judge right and wrong. Your conscience provides you with right judgment and courage to do what is right regardless of the personal consequences.

To conclude this section, I would like to return to the perceptions of Siobhan, who earlier explained that her position was altered inside and outside the drama when she role-played as the father of the protagonist. It illustrates the phenomenon I described in Chapter 1 – that is, the particular strength of process drama to invite tension and contradiction, and help students work within the ambiguities in a collective but not nec-

essarily consensual process. Siobhan began the work with a sophisticated and strong opinion about the dilemma at hand, and so her understanding at the conclusion of the work has particular import. She explains:

> Kelly Turner's story was based on what is right and what is wrong. Unfortunately, everyone seems to have a different opinion as to the true definition of these words. We are all raised in different environments, thus causing our morals and values to differ from those around us. Her story has taught me that everyone's definition is right in its own way. It may not always seem that way to you, but you cannot force a person to change their beliefs. Her story has also taught me that in nearly every situation the 'right' thing does not always seem to apply to everyone. There is usually the right thing for you and the right thing for someone else. It is always your choice to decide from which point of view you are going to look at a situation.

The 'Kelly Turner' story was not a story that the students heard about and forgot; it was a story that they worked with, manipulated, symbolically represented, and lived inside over some two weeks. It posed important questions about what is 'right' and asked students to think about difficult questions. The real strength of working through process drama with students is that they can live, however briefly, inside a fiction that engages who they are, where they come from, and how they might like to proceed. Spontaneous role-play requires higher thinking, reflection, and an accommodation of old and new ideas that challenge our thinking. Schools need to make more, not less, time in the curriculum for these kinds of extended explorations of important human/humanizing questions.

Next, I would like to recount another process drama in an attempt to re-create for the reader the 'living through' curriculum of drama education. The story of 'Philip Malloy' also drew on students' role-playing and story-building skills to reach new understandings that undoubtedly have significant implications in their 'real' lives.

'Philip Malloy'

Avi's story *Nothing But the Truth* (1991) is written in scenes in scripted form and recounts the story of a ninth-grade boy who causes a disturbance in his classroom by 'singing' along with the national anthem when it is played over the school public address system, to the dismay of his teacher. This simple disagreement escalates to the point where school district officials, parents, politicians, and the press become involved in the 'stand-off' between teacher and student. I would like to describe two different role-playing conventions used with the students that illustrate a broadening in understanding of character and situation. This fiction, set in a high school, was not very far removed from the students' actual world, which they called on readily in their role-playing work.

Dramatic Structures II

The first convention used to generate the created world and deepen the drama work is called 'forum theatre,' used commonly by drama teachers and others, such as drama therapists, political theatre activists, or conflict-mediation experts, who also use role-playing in their work. Neelands (1990, 37) describes forum theatre as follows: 'a situation (chosen by the group to illuminate a topic or experience relevant to the drama) is enacted by a small group whilst the others observe.' Both the role-players and the observers are involved in creating the 'world'; however, observers can stop the role-playing at any time and alter the action or refocus it if they feel it has lost authenticity. Observers are also able to step in and take over roles if they choose to add new ideas. In other words, as educator Dorothy Heathcote (1984a) has described, those watching as audience in drama are not there to be entertained but are participants engaged in the struggle to understand the teaching/learning dynamic.

During this drama, students in all five classes chose to explore in greater depth the scene in the book between Philip and the

assistant principal, using the convention of forum theatre. In this scripted scene, Philip is suspended for his undesirable behaviour. As these scenes were worked through using improvisation, it was evident to all that the students who took on the role of principal throughout the scene-building were drawing on their experiences of authority in schools. Their language, gestures, and arguments all expressed a strong sense of the characters involved. Students imitate their teachers with frightening precision. Because the forum theatre convention was very useful for exploring the two sides of the story, students in three of the classes asked to set up a new scene, using forum theatre, of a meeting between Philip and the teacher herself in order to further establish the two clashing viewpoints. Of this role-playing exercise, Katarina observed:

> The same incident (singing the national anthem) seemed like two completely different stories when the basic facts are interpreted by the two parties differently or when one party lies. In Philip Malloy/Miss Narwin's situation, I feel that they both perhaps overexaggerated a tad. Maybe Philip did more though, considering he didn't want to get in trouble. Basically this scenario could happen quite easily. Facts get mixed up all the time. Our memories/interpretations are never really completely accurate.

In the case of this story, students – many of whom have had similar encounters with authority figures in the school – used this tool to examine a familiar situation in this 'once-removed' way and to formulate new understandings about human communication. When I asked the girls how the same incident (singing the national anthem) seemed like two completely different stories, many drew on actual experiences of this kind in their lives and arrived at new conclusions. Ana said:

> I know. Trust me. People really believe that what they say is the truth. In actuality, probably none of their stories was the absolute truth. After a while you start to believe what you think happened and it becomes the truth.

There were many realizations of this kind throughout the role-playing, as students attempted to 'get into the skin' of the two protagonists. Much learning happens in classrooms when students have the space to reflect upon encounters at some distance. Latoya reflected on the 'versions' of stories we encountered:

> I recall discussing this very topic in class one day and someone said that there are always three sides to every story. I find this to be very true. A person's story always seems to make them look good and make the other party involved look bad. The same thing is true in this case. Philip's story makes him look completely innocent. He nearly destroyed the career of a well-respected teacher. On the other hand, Miss Narwin's story made Philip look like he was causing an enormous disturbance in class. In this case she was the victim. In Philip's story he was the victim. The large difference between these two stories was that Philip's version became 'front page news.' No one cared much about Miss Narwin's perspective and this gave Philip the upper hand. The true story must lie somewhere in the middle. This example shows how one story always seems to have several versions.

I used a second role-playing device in the 'Philip Malloy' drama. A structure called 'hot-seating,' as described by Neelands (1990, 28), can serve to highlight a character's motivations and personality, can encourage insights into relationships among attitudes and events and how events affect attitudes, as well as provide an opportunity to develop reflective awareness of human behaviour. In this case the class, working as themselves, had the opportunity to question or interview the role-player, who remained 'in character.' In each class I began the interrogation of the student being hot-seated, but, as the video-taped lessons reveal, it was not long before the questions were coming at the role-player from all directions in the room. There had been, at this point in the drama, a palpable investment in the character of Philip, expressed by students both collectively and individually. In reflecting on this process with the classes, it

seemed as though their learning was tied in with a classmate's interpretation of a role:

When Beth role-played as Philip, I learned through her interpretation that he was quite cocky and arrogant. He seemed quite sure of himself. Beth also played Philip with attitude and self-assurance. Philip to me was very quick-witted and clever in the way he returned his answers with references from the book. Through Beth, I saw Philip as a pretty typical teenager. (Erin)

Sandy also remarked on the resonance she felt with Beth's interpretation:

Beth did a great job when she portrayed Philip as the nonchalant 'I haven't a care in the world' kind of guy. Philip (Beth) came across as a selfish, self-absorbed teenager whose sole purpose in life is to make trouble for others. Maybe I'm being a little harsh, but so was he. He didn't look scared or intimidated, he looked like he was going to stick to his story. The teasing and humorous side shined through. His defence was that Miss Narwin needed to lighten up. He looked as if he didn't care if Miss Narwin got hurt. I think we experienced a darker side of Philip with Beth's portrayal.

What is interesting in this student's reflection is her seamless movement between Beth the 'actor' and Philip the 'character,' all the while illustrating that her classmate's interpretation had furthered her understanding of the events and the character.

Beth, reflecting on her own work, also demonstrates a certain 'artistic licence' or authorship that grew out of her initial understanding of the character. She explains:

When I role-played as Philip I tried to portray him the way I saw him. I think Philip was the kind of person who always thought he was right and would do anything for a laugh. Even though I can't remember what I did, I think I tried to act as if I didn't care because I was right and I also tried to crack a few jokes. Also,

because Philip was stubborn, arrogant and wanted to prove that he wasn't loud, I came up with the term 'HUM-SING.'

Often built into drama lessons are opportunities for students to step outside and look in, to replay the events of a story in reflective writing within the drama. In the 'Philip Malloy' drama, I took several opportunities throughout the process to build individual reflective writing into the created world. In these cases, I contrived a purpose for writing inside the drama and provided the imagined audience for the letter writing. The students were aware, from the actual story, that the teacher, Miss Narwin, had a sister who lived in Florida who was a kind of confidante to her. This letter writing asked students to select content and adopt appropriate registers and viewpoints in writing personal letters. This served as a means of reviewing the context and further developing character. Many letters integrated previous details about the character's life, and several found a 'voice' in their writing that was very different from their own. Isabel wrote:

Dear Anita,
How are you? I myself am not too fine. You'll never guess what has happened. Remember I told you about that boy in my class, Philip Malloy, the one who is very disruptive. He got suspended for two days because of his constant mocking of our national anthem. Philip, every morning, would belt out the 'Star Spangled Banner,' even though he knows it's against the rules, so I had to excuse him from my class. But somehow the story has gone public and the media is now involved. Why, just yesterday there was an article in the *Manchester Record* about it. They made me out to be a horrible old witch with no compassion. Oh Anita, it was just awful. The entire article was bogus. I mean even Philip's grade was wrong. But I'm worried still. I know that people believe what they read. My reputation is tarnished after all these years. I am at a loss. I don't know what to do!
Love, Peg

Other students decided to invent their own audience and style

of writing, some choosing to send telegrams such as the following:

To: Philip Malloy
I am writing to you from the Kids Speak Out Association, and let me tell you that there should be more kids like you. You are a major idol to millions of kids in the United States as well as around the world. I applaud you for your extreme patriotism towards the United States of America.
Shirley Macleaud, Kids Speak Out Association
Aurora, Illinois

I use these examples to make the point that drama offers students a very particular kind of writing experience. I cannot count how many times I have provided the English as a Second Language teacher with impressive examples of writing skills from some of his students who, in a contextualized and sometimes charged drama, have expressed themselves with more passion, clarity, and eloquence than they have been able to unleash before. Booth (1994) says the process of writing can be a language form in which engaged writers/participants explore their feelings and ideas, learning not only to express themselves but to rethink, reassess, restructure, and re-examine their work and possibly even come to an understanding of the needs of the reader. As with the manipulation of the theatrical medium, students begin to see themselves as writers or 'characters in writing' controlling the medium. Booth (1994) explains further:

Today's writing curricula stress the active use of writing rather than exercises about the act of writing. In some classrooms, traditional motivations for writing have not dealt with inner compulsion or need, but only with the completion of creative writing tasks. I have found that when writing is embedded in context that has a personal significance for the writer, the writing skills themselves will be enhanced. If children are engaged in the expressive and reflective aspects of drama, living through, 'here and now' experiences that draw upon their own life meanings, then the

writing that accompanies the drama and the writing that grows out of it may possess the same characteristics and qualities. (123)

I would like to look now at two dramas that reveal the kind of collective process students experience in a drama class. Once again, drama structures are used to slow down, repeat, negotiate, and renegotiate meaning among participants in their created world.

Drama as Collective Process

'Maudie-Ann'

In this drama 'forum theatre' was used to provide a structure in which students could dream up together the details of the context of their created world. This structure in particular, as it is used in much drama work and as it was employed here, has the effect of slowing down and drawing out students' creations of character and context. It is also an example of the collective negotiation of meaning that, in my view, is the mainstay of drama education. Much attention is given to consensus forming in many educational contexts, but forum theatre work, as employed in my grade 10 curriculum, is largely uninterested in consensus. Instead, drama is deeply invested in collective meaning-making, understood less for its uniformity of voices and more for its multiplicity of voices.

I began the 'Maudie-Ann' story by inviting students to spontaneously improvise crew people on a voyage, acting, myself, as the 'captain' of our ship. As captain, I alluded to a character called Maudie-Ann, who was the captain's daughter. After some discussions about our duties on this large ship, we came out of role and I asked the students to re-create theatrically a series of letters, choosing the conventions and elements of form in which they now had some expertise. I produced the collection of letters from a book written and illustrated by Catherine Brighton entitled *Dearest Grandmama*. The letters are all set in the year 1830, written by an 11-year-old girl to her grandmother. The letters tell

of a young girl's adventures at sea with her father, the captain of a ship. In the letters, the girl speaks of a friend called the 'silent boy' whom she relies on and trusts until his mysterious disappearance one day.

This brief introduction set up our context for group work in forum theatre. In this case, the forum theatre convention was used as a means of solving the mystery of the young girl's turn for the worse after the disappearance of her 'silent boy' friend. I began by playing the father, with a student playing the daughter, while the rest of the class watched and interrupted, changing the course of the scene as it unfolded. In all of the five classes, students frequently interrupted the role-playing in order to offer suggestions about 'how it should be done.' There was obvious disagreement in the room about the nature of the relationship between father and daughter, about the real or fictitious character of the silent boy, about the appropriateness or inappropriateness of the behaviour of the daughter or father. What can be understood from the students' work as 'participant-actors,' or 'participant-audience' as I like to call them, was their collective commitment to try out, rehearse, or replay different possibilities. As the role-playing proceeded in each class, different students offered suggestions by entering the scene and tapping one of the two players on the shoulder in order to replace them in the scene. Frequently, students would change their minds about how something should have gone, and with a simple move out of role, we could, as a group, discuss alternate possibilities. What results is an obvious collection of ideas that fill in the details of the characters and the scenario by a continuous adjustment of adding in, taking away, rehearsing, and re-rehearsing possibilities.

Part of the strength of this kind of collective process is its inclusion of voices and its overt position that there is not just one way to experience a story. It is not a clean, fast, or direct movement to a conclusion. It is slow and meandering in its progress. Opinions are strong and strongly held, but the process resembles a slow drawing out of ideas and suggestions that begin to come together because of the differently held views in the room.

As a result, the 'final product' is a collage of ideas and images. The characters are multidimensional, the context collectively imagined. Students enter into role at their own pace and in their own way.

Christine Warner's (1997) study on the nature of engagement in drama identifies how students are engaged in their work in several ways that have to do with more than vocal contributions. Beyond the 'Talkers,' in her research on the nature of students' engagement in drama, she identifies groups she has called 'Processors,' 'Participant Observers,' and 'Listeners/Outsiders.' Possibly the greatest contribution of her study is its evidence that engagement processes are elaborate and usually begin before there is public evidence of that engagement. Through systematic study of classroom drama, she has found evidence that supports what drama teachers have believed for a long time: most participants in drama, whether they are vocal or not, begin their intricate mental operations leading up to actual engagement in drama activities before there is any public evidence of these operations.

Morgan and Saxton (1987) defined a Taxonomy of Personal Engagement based on the physical and/or verbal appearance of participation in drama, citing five active ways of identifying engagement in a drama activity:

1. Acquiescence in being involved: evidenced by participation in a congruent, appropriate, and supportive manner.
2. Willingness to engage: agreement to operate 'as if'; the suspension of disbelief.
3. Relating: agreement to accept others, places, and objects into the imagined world.
4. Identifying: agreement to endow the role with self, summoning past experience to the demands of the present dramatic situation.
5. Evaluating: satisfaction in the experience.

According to the authors, drama operates within two frames: the expressive frame and the meaning frame; or the outer mani-

festation and the inner understanding. The authors insist further that drama, in its most satisfying form, can only be realized when the inner world of meaning is connected to the outer world of expressive action. In my experience, however, it is obvious that not all students in a class make a verbal or physical contribution to the collective work, but that this does not mean that there is no development in their inner world of meaning. In our work in the 'Maudie-Ann' story, students who did not actively participate in the forum theatre, by either interrupting the scenes to make contributions or by replacing players in the scenes, had certainly participated in the building of the world in what we might describe as a more private way that, nonetheless, took account of others' more vocal participation. They had certainly not 'opted out' in their silence, but rather had begun a process of accommodation of the ideas and perspectives in the room. This silence, whether actively chosen or part of a self-censoring, is not so much a gender phenomenon, but is, in this context, more connected to language ability and culture. There are common myths about 'talkers' and 'nontalkers' in classrooms, but I have found this to be a much more sophisticated issue. Facility with language, confidence, and culture are strong determinants of participation and clearly affect students' perceptions of self and other in this single-sex classroom.

Often it is in drama writing work in the classroom that teachers become aware of the less obvious participation going on at any given time in a classroom. In the 'Maudie-Ann' story, the students were asked to write in role as Maudie-Ann, projecting themselves ten years into the future. It was apparent that students who had been silent during the forum theatre work were participant-audience as opposed to participant-actors, as they had integrated a good deal of the detail of the character and scene-building, adding to this their own ingredients in the writing exercise. Natasha, a particularly shy student in one class, had been silent during the collective forum theatre work, although in her writing she revealed an obvious engagement with the story and an accommodation of others' more vocal contributions:

1840
Dear Diary,
It's been 10 years since the voyage ended. I'm now 21 and I still feel empty inside like when I was 11 and the silent boy disappeared. I still remember him like it was yesterday. His sad, strange, and silent image remains in my head. Papa tried to understand so many times and yet he couldn't. I try not to mention the boy to my father so he won't get upset, but I still miss him. He was my friend, he saved my life and he also listened to me even though he did not answer back. I wonder if I'm ever going to see him again. I hope I do and I also hope he talks more. I have to leave for now but I'll be back.
Maudie-Ann

Writing can also be an intimidating aspect of school life for those with difficulty in verbal expression. As a drama teacher, I am always acutely aware of those students who find a voice in their writing-in-role that is easily heard beyond the errors in spelling and sentence structure. Many students are more comfortable with oral expression than with written expression, but I have found that, even among those students with obvious difficulty with the written word, drama can feature a context in a way that encourages them to connect with their own internal motivation to write. Rulanda is a new Canadian who had been in the country two years and was, for the second year, in the introductory level of English as a second language in the school. I asked the students to take on the role of Maudie-Ann at age 21, but before they began writing, Rulanda approached me to ask whether she could write as the captain rather than the girl. This, in itself, was rather remarkable as Rulanda hardly spoke in class and was often embarrassed by her weakness in English. Her diary entry suggested a level of understanding and responsiveness to the story that may have gone undetected without this writing exercise. She wrote:

Dear Diary,
last ten years my daughter didn't ate two days because she wants

to talk to the ghost. I can't really forget it I want to talk to her about the ghost but she not talking to me. Why can she talk to me? does she love the ghost more than me? I remembered that she telling me about what she doing in her school. Now she can't talked to me about this silent boy. How will I push her to talk to me? I hope this silent boy will show to my daughter and tell her that I love her very much more than anything in the world. I hope someday before I dye I will see him.
From: Father
P.S. I hope she love me.

Student engagement in drama can be a complex and elusive matter. The work in the 'Maudie-Ann' story revealed how participation is not a simple matter of answering the questions when students are invited to draw on their actual world experiences and speak from the voice that is most accessible to them. But participation in all its complexities is a crucial subject for teachers as it often figures prominently in student assessment. To summarize, drama as a collective process is not about consensus, but an accommodation of perspectives and a collectivity of ideas. It is not an easy or swift process, but one that relies on and is enhanced by the collective negotiation of meaning. This collective negotiating process is important in a drama classroom because there are many kinds of engagement, many levels of ability, indeed many realities operating in that classroom at any given time. As Trudy the 'bag lady' in Jane Wagner's (1986) play *The Search for Signs of Intelligent Life in the Universe* declares, 'reality is nothin' but a collective hunch.' A combination of oral and written activities seems to provide students with different entry points into the work so they can simultaneously be attentive to the creativity of their classmates and their own imaginative processes within the larger-group process.

'Kerry Smith'

'Kerry Smith' is a dramatic story about a teenage girl arrested and charged with the abduction of an infant. Our drama begins

once the child is safely returned to his parents. This drama context used a newspaper headline as the trigger, or 'way in.' Few details, therefore, of the protagonist's life were known as the class set out to build a context and collectively create the character of Kerry. Drama structures that supported the 'what happens when' approach previously discussed were used in order to pull together the various perspectives in the room. After asking the students to engage in several brief role-playing exercises in pairs (as the parents of the abducted child in conversation; the arresting officer and his or her captain; the defence lawyer and the police sergeant), the classes decided that they would like to get into the head of Kerry herself. This moment illustrates further the collective process of the group.

They decided that they would like to use the 'interview' structure, playing the investigating police officers in the case. Although one student played Kerry while another played the investigator, as in the forum theatre mode discussed earlier, all other students were imagined to be behind a one-way mirror with devices that allowed them to communicate with the officer interrogating Kerry. In this way, the task of eliciting responses belonged to the class as a whole.

The first of the five classes to work on this drama seemed quite determined to 'create' the character of 'Kerry' as a working-class, unconfident, teenage girl, and I was troubled by the ease with which this character depiction came to them. My quick decision to keep Kerry silent in the interview, therefore, was one of the ways in which I began to slow down the work in order that students might move beyond stereotype and be challenged in their thinking about the character and her motives. The student who was to play Kerry, then, was given private instructions not to speak in the interview.

The question of stereotypes is an important one for drama teachers who are interested in more than reinforcing gender, class, and racial inequalities, because stereotypes have a very powerful hold on the imaginations of most teenagers. For instance, one of the earliest explanations of ways in which boys' and girls' interests begin to separate out in the early years of

schooling was explored in the concept of sex-role stereotyping (Millard, 1997). In my single-sex setting, however, it seems that prescribed stereotypes of class and race are more likely to emerge in the delineation of characters. Therefore, in order to help students move beyond sweeping generalizations and facile conclusions, filtering what they see through their own built-in lenses of personal reference, I made a choice, as teacher, to pro-long the 'living inside' the narrative in order to draw out from students more thoughtful meanings. After the results I saw in the first class, I repeated this particular limitation of the 'silent Kerry' in the other four classes because I was impressed by how hard the students worked to offer alternatives and dig deeper in this 'investigative process' when the obvious or predictable answers were not forthcoming.

Drama must also take seriously the idea that each group includes individuals at their own stage of development. Drama in education can offer a more level playing field for students who might otherwise be limited to their particular academic stream; there never has to be a definitive way to experience the story. Still, the drama teacher must be conscious of students' predispositions toward stereotypical responses in working through imaginative and improvised play. Stereotypical and hegemonic responses can be very powerful in a classroom and can often disempower individual students. One way to move beyond these more limiting contributions when working in a group is to be conscious that when you are building narratives you must know where the drama is 'living' at any given time; in effect, you are simultaneously constructing and deconstruct-ing. Jonathon Neelands (1984) observes that this constitutes a dialectical rather than a didactic form of learning. If the work is merely plot driven, sequential, 'what happens next,' then surely the stronger, more confident students, those with cul-tural capital, will monopolize the work. But the 'what happens when' approach does not fix you to a previous happening and does not require the 'best' or most obvious idea to come for-ward. When students feel that they can make an individual contribution to the whole, the pressure is off and the tensions

of varying perspectives co-exist. Most often the responses are deepened when the drive forward is about shaping, altering, adjusting, and drawing out, and not about arriving at the next juncture.

Again in student reflections, many commented on the learning they experienced by working together as 'investigators': 'When we were investigators, it helped me understand the character better because I was able to see other people's points of view,' said Kristin. Emerita offered, 'It helped the understanding of Kerry's life better because we were able to see other people's points of view on Kerry's life.'

As in the 'Maudie-Ann' drama, a kind of negotiating process in the meaning-making was explicit in the work; and structures, sometimes chosen by the group and sometimes imposed by the teacher, helped the students explore and possibly move beyond easy or stereotypical solutions to problems. My aim to introduce structures that would result in more considered responses from students was clarified early on in the process by the reactions I was seeing from students. 'Maybe she was poor and her parents didn't love her enough,' offered Josie in our initial discussions. 'Maybe she was going to lie to her boyfriend and pretend it was hers so he would marry her.' With these initial responses, which may make for good soap-opera storylines, I decided to try, instead, to ensure that the role-playing work could allow for new insights to be developed within a framework of constraints. Neelands (1990) suggests that 'context-building action and the controlled pace of reflective action may produce challenges to assumptions and prejudices' (74). And so for the drama teacher, too, the process is always challenging if we set as a goal the commitment to include all voices, all the while striving for new ways to see or hear a problem.

Drama as Personal Development

The last of the four areas of learning is an important one for drama educators and those interested in the curricular possibilities of drama education. It illustrates drama as a teaching and

learning process. For example, a student's personal response to fictional narratives exemplifies the relationship of the learner to dominant modes of thinking. Literacy movements and early instruction in both reading and writing have, in the last decade, insisted upon students' personal response to reading and writing as central to the acquisition of these skills (Wells 1987; Millard 1997). Drama education, too, relies on this interaction of personal response with fiction, and, because of this, has been used in many schools to raise consciousness and 'teach' social issues. I would add to this a particular potential of drama education to offer girls discursive practices in which they can enter the classroom work as subject. In her studies in co-educational settings, Walkerdine (1990) has provided evidence for the ways in which discursive practices in the classroom can render children either powerful or powerless. The classroom setting is not a neutral space in relation to positions of power. Drama structures have an opportunity, therefore, to intervene in spaces normally advantageous to boys and offer the possibility for alternative discursive patterns to be tested.

'Earthwoman'

We began a drama that was rooted in a fantastical world of native folklore. The story I used as a source was a picture book by Jane Mobley entitled *Starhusband* (1979). The story became, once again, the springboard into the action the students began to create. This particular story tells of a young native girl who, after dreaming of a 'star' husband in the sky, finds herself transported to the sky, where she finds her beautiful starhusband. Before long, she and her husband have a child, who is the Moon. The Earthwoman, who is nameless in this community of sky-dwellers, soon finds herself bored by her lack of participation in this new community life, unlike on earth, where she had dug for roots to help the healers in the community. She longed to see her 'earth' family, but more importantly she began to feel her 'difference' among the sky-dwellers. Although she had a good relationship with her husband, one night, against his wishes, she

dug a hole in the floor of the sky to catch a small glimpse of the family she left behind.

By developing the story, again using many of Neeland's (1990) drama structures to frame the work, the students take the story where they will, by uncovering issues and concerns they choose to explore. Of course, every time a drama source is used, the worlds created vary, because different students build the story in different ways. There are, however, common themes that an experienced teacher begins to identify as questions of particular import to grade 10 students in a context like ours. I shall comment on a few of these concerns in the discussion of this work.

As a feminist actively engaged in the emancipation of girls and women, I was keenly aware of the patriarchal and hetero-sexist assumptions of the source and therefore determined to validate the subjectivities of all the girls in the class, including those whose life experiences or choices were not immediately reflected in the imagery of the story. Some may simply not choose a source with such potential to reinforce unliberated or deterministic roles for women, but it is my view that difficult sources ought to be used so that students have the opportunity to defamiliarize and thereby render explicit what often remain familiar, unchallenged, and prescriptive images. It was first in whole-group, out-of-role discussions where I realized the potential for this fantastical story to become a metaphor in ways I had not anticipated.

It was not surprising that in this story many students strongly identified with the concept of 'not fitting in.' Natasha, a bi-racial student, was the first to pull the focus of the story to a discussion of racially mixed marriages. 'You're not black and you're not white. My mother says I'm lucky I'm both. Yeah right.' Suddenly we became involved in a conversation about culturally or racially mixed unions. Next came a contribution from Lily, a Portuguese-Canadian girl, who again shifted the focus of our discussion: 'Two different cultures never work. Besides, my father would kill me if I married a guy who wasn't Portuguese.' Following this was a discussion of 'home' and where that is when you are an 'immigrant.' I was aware of the

texture of the story that we were beginning to weave and well aware of those we were excluding in our discussion that assumed the inevitability of marriage within a heterosexual framework and the biological determinism of motherhood. Often drama teachers, as part of their larger role in the process, choose to inject the voices we are not hearing in the room. The masks we wear allow us to do this. While personal sharing was quite common in these drama classrooms, I was aware that the world of fiction was our necessary mediator for any further exploration that might include the sometimes problematic actual worlds of the students.

The story-making continued. After a disagreement with her husband about the nature of her discontent (using the convention of forum theatre), the husband insists that she should never again destroy the floor of the sky and that she should find comfort in her new life in the sky, which she herself chose. As imagined by the students (for this is now their story), Earthwoman makes a painful decision (this was arrived at after lively discussions in the room) to ask permission of the Counsel of Elders in the sky to grant her the right to leave the sky world and return to her homeland. Of course, they conclude, she must leave her son the Moon behind, because his role in the sky is far too important.

Critical Incident

I would like to recount a critical incident that occurred in one of the grade 10 classes as an arresting example of the kind of personal development for which drama education is often an instrument. After three days of getting to this point in the story in one class, I informed the students that the next day we would be staging this meeting of the elders to decide if and under what conditions we would allow the Earthwoman to leave. This structure of the 'meeting,' as described by Neelands (1990), emphasizes negotiation and the 'need to balance individual needs and interests with other people's' (24). It was this 'meeting' that would take us to the next place in our invented story.

At the beginning of the next class period, Madeline approached me as I was taking attendance, to ask whether, before we began the 'meeting,' she could read aloud a letter she had written as a counsel member to the Earthwoman. As a teacher I had a dual reaction to this request. On the one hand, I was delighted that Madeline had produced an unsolicited piece of writing. This demonstrated a rather sophisticated level of belief in role and engagement in our work. On the other hand, however, I felt the need to protect Madeline from any of her peers who had not necessarily entered into the story to the same extent as she obviously had. I asked Madeline to save her letter until we began the meeting, knowing she would be much 'safer' inside the created world. What followed was very gratifying, although I did not realize the full implications of Madeline's actions until days later. Madeline read her letter, in role, to the student playing the Earthwoman on this particular day. It was a letter of advice to the Earthwoman that, while claiming to understand her reasons for leaving, pleaded with her never to forget her son, the Moon, to explain to him clearly that he is not to blame for her leaving, and to promise always to be in touch with him as long as she lived. It was a moving letter. We carried on in role and, in fact, brought the story to a close with a ritualized 'leaving ceremony' where other students came forward too with their spontaneous 'words of wisdom' for the Earthwoman.

The following two days, Madeline was not in class. She came back to class after that, but only to tell me that she was very sorry but had dropped out of school because she had to move to Nova Scotia with her mother. I was very sorry to see Madeline leave the class. The following day I went to her guidance counsellor to confirm the story and perhaps learn some more details. There I discovered that Madeline had been coming only to drama class for several weeks and they had not been bothering her about that because she had been, according to her counsellor, suicidal when she was in grade 9, and was coming from a very troubled background. It seems her mother, a battered woman and an alcoholic, had one month earlier left for Nova Scotia to be with her abusive boyfriend. The counsellor was

under the impression that Madeline had decided to stay in Toronto and live with a grandmother. Suddenly and rather painfully, the letter made much more sense. Madeline had left to find her mother. Although there is no way to confirm this, I was left to think that our drama was barely an abstraction, coming disturbingly close to Madeline's own struggles. This fantasy story, for no particular reason that I might have predicted, had, in fact, ignited the concerns and passions of several students. The structures we used set up the 'once removed' space of fiction that challenged them to take ownership for the kinds of things they felt they needed to question both in our story-building and, in some cases, in their lives.

To return to Natasha, the student for whom the story was about identity and mixed racial backgrounds, I close with the letter she wrote (possibly echoing her own mother) in a final writing-in-role exercise after her class as the 'Council of Elders' had come to the decision that the Earthwoman should be allowed to leave. Natasha wrote:

Dear Son,
I'm writing this letter to let you know how much I love you and how much I want only the best for you.

I know right now you are too young to comprehend what is going on with me, with your father and everything else. I hope when you are of age you will understand where I am coming from and why I am leaving the sky world.

Son, ever since I came to the sky world, it hasn't been anything like I expected, actually it has been the total opposite. You are my salvation. When I wished to be a sky-dweller, I pictured fulfilment, peace of mind and happiness. I find my happiness in you, every time you smile, you make me smile. You are my world. I want you to always know that you're always in my heart, now and forever.

My leaving is the best thing for everyone. A mortal girl doesn't belong in the sky. Although I am mortal please don't condemn me for it no matter what anyone might say. Don't forget you are half of me, you are half human. This isn't something to put you down,

it makes you unique. You shine brighter than anything else in
every way. Most importantly you are my star shining in my soul
for all time.
Your mother
with much love

A story like this one certainly draws attention to the ideolo-
gies and assumptions of our own cultures and circumstances.
Although in the classrooms we had arrived at what might be
described as a 'closure' for our invented world, it was important
that I remain aware of the kind of dissonance this closure might
have produced for some. I chose a final writing exercise that
might open up the possibility for students to 'write their own
ending' and finish the story in a satisfying way for them. Many
students needed to write her back up to the sky, happy with her
child and husband. They depicted the earth as an inhospitable
or changed place: 'She held her son and her husband and she
knew she was where she belonged. She was home.' Others had
the moon coming to get her at her death:

There was a bright light walking towards the old woman's house.
When people opened their eyes again the boy and the old woman
were gone. The people noticed that the moon had mysteriously
reappeared, but something was different about it. The villagers
noticed that the moon had a face of a young woman smiling at the
face of the boy who had disappeared with the wise woman, shining brighter than ever in the sky.

Many had her return to the sky, but others had her 'die in peace'
on earth. All endings were possible as students took on the role,
this time, of author.

The point of drama education is not to transmit a particular
ideology or to leave unchallenged the things we think we
believe, but to see anew, understand ourselves more fully,
expand our thinking, and understand how that thinking has
been shaped by our social positions. It is an opening-up process
that must, at all costs, leave open the possibilities of alternative

ways to see or hear or live the story. It is a process of alienation in the tradition of Brecht – that is, drama education, too, has the potential to set life up as a site for struggle and change. It can be explicitly concerned with the deconstructing and reconstructing process when we alienate representations of gender, class, and race. It is one means of dismantling seductive, stereotypical images, of resisting the limited and limiting discursive and aesthetic representations of self/other. In drama, we can have a depiction of character that is insufficient and open, that can be explored using drama conventions to create alternative aesthetic expressions. These are the kinds of critical incidents and classroom stories that supply drama teachers with much evidence about the kind of personal growth and understanding that might happen within and through the drama curriculum.

In the next chapter, I would like to share the particular choices I made as a researcher of my own classroom and provide a closer look at the students whose insights have changed the way I see the processes of learning.

Chapter Three

Research in the Classroom

In the midst of a preoccupation with the measurable, with benchmarks and outcomes, new voices are becoming audible in the world of education. They are voices responsive to the talk of the 'reflective practitioner,' to novel modes of participant observation in actual classrooms, to the judgements of practitioners asked to think about their own thinking.

Maxine Greene, 'Foreword,' *Researching Drama and Arts Education:*
Paradigms and Possibilities (1996)

Personal Narrative and Self-Construction

The thrilling and critical task of 'deconstruction' began after our several months of working in role, creating worlds, and writing and thinking about those worlds. We began by talking about selfhood when I asked the girls how they see themselves in the drama class, as compared with their other classes. Of the nineteen students interviewed, seventeen saw themselves as 'very different' in drama class compared with their other classes in the school. Their explanations of the reasons for this difference clustered around two general themes. The first had to do with the more informal or relaxed setting of the drama class that allowed them to 'express feelings' and be 'more yourself':

Dahlia: Uh yeah. I don't know. Drama's fun ... it's really fun. It's more relaxing than other classes.
KG: So you like that it's more informal?

Dahlia: Yeah, it's good. Drama I talk more, give a lot more opinions.

Sandy elaborated on the 'difference' she feels in drama class:

Sandy: Yeah because in drama class you can act, how ... you ... like you know in other classes you just sit down at a desk and write off the board but in drama class you really get into what you're doing.
KG: Is there a down side to that?
Sandy: Sometimes when you're like, shy and stuff but at the end of the semester you feel better, I guess.
KG: Do you personally feel like you've made progress?
Sandy: Uh huh.

The second theme to which several students made reference in explaining why they feel they behave/participate differently in drama had to do with their sense of the 'group.' Juanita commented: 'Yeah, I say more 'cause everyone's involved ... you're not just sitting down copying stuff. You're doing stuff more in this class than in other classes.' Melissa elaborated: 'Yeah it's like more open and everybody talks. In other classes it's just work, work, work.' On that particular point, Danielle explains:

Well yeah in a way 'cause you just feel you can be more yourself. It's not like, 'OK do this, do that, do this, do that.' It's more like everybody works together. In other classes it's more independent, but in drama it's like everybody works together.

I decided to probe further by asking, 'Do you think there are characteristics or aspects of yourself and your life experiences that you brought into the dramas we worked on together?' When I asked this question, some students chose to answer with specific references to one of the dramas we had worked on, while others responded in a more general way. But there emerged three general categories into which the students' responses fell. The three categories that encompass the responses of all students have to do with their 'feelings,' with 'issues' they face in their lives, and with

their 'value systems.' Two students make particular reference to our drama where 'the girl felt like an outsider.'

> Lynn: Yeah, I think so. The first story where she was left out and kind of a loner.
> KG: You related to that?
> Lynn: Yeah a lot.

Natalie explained: 'I guess Maudie-Ann being sort of an outsider, I guess. Yeah I did.'

Lily made reference to our 'Kelly Turner' drama (in which there are several racist characters) when she described how she is affected by racism in her daily life:

> Lily: Probably because I've been in a similar situation 'cause of where I live. 'Cause I live in an Irish area and I went to a party with a bunch of Irish friends and these guys are like 'Is she Latin? Is she dirty?' And I was like 'no I'm Portuguese' and they're like 'OK you can stay then.' Yeah really, like, big time racist there.
> KG: So you related in some way to our Kelly Turner drama?
> Lily: I seen them beat up on so many people and you keep your mouth shut 'cause you know you would be the next one.

Christina, referencing another drama, articulated quite clearly the 'adjustment' of integrating her 'home' culture with the North American culture she faced after immigrating:

> Christina: Yeah, Earthwoman, she went up to the sky and she didn't know anything about it. She had to, in a way, adjust to the whole environment and that's what happened to me when I got to Canada ... um ... I didn't know how to talk. I didn't know anybody 'cause everybody's customs are different.
> KG: And has that changed at all for you now?
> Christina: Well, by going to school you become aware of everything around you. You get in with it.
> KG: You understand the culture more?
> Christina: Yeah.

KG: Do you think you've lost any aspects of your own culture?
Christina: Not at all. At home we talk our language and we're really involved in the community. I mean, I am who I am and I'm not gonna change that. I'm Portuguese.

Many of the girls made reference to their 'values' and reiterated how they bring themselves, or parts of themselves, to the characters they create:

Graciella: Well it was easy [to bring myself into it] 'cause like with Mary Morgan I really felt it, 'cause, like, I'm really against abortion ... I don't know ... So like the way I felt really got me into the character.
KG: You mean your values?
Graciella: Yes, yes.

Marcella, who also identified with the character of Mary Morgan, the poor servant girl, explained:

Oh, like Mary Morgan. I thought that was such a good story 'cause it's like my family. 'You can't have a boyfriend, you can't do this, you can't do that' and all this stuff. And I think, well what if something accidentally happens? What if I accidentally get pregnant. There were so many different, interesting characters ... like how everyone acted and it was just so good and so ... dramatic.

Two students, in particular, commented on the process of bringing themselves into their role-playing:

Fenny: Yeah, 'cause you take all of *your* surroundings and you use that to make the character. Yeah, I think that the character you play is always a part of you, like even though you could be playing something totally opposite.
KG: Yeah, that's a good point.

Nicole reflected on this same theme with particular reference, again, to our drama that addressed questions of racism:

Nicole: In some of them yeah ... like ... in the one we did, Kelly
Turner. Like, that's how I would respond if it was my friend.
KG: What parts of yourself did you bring to that?
Nicole: Like, my attitude towards things.

Ciara was the only student who suggested that she did not
draw on parts of herself in creating characters, and this was of
particular interest to me as she, unlike the previous two students, is white:

Ciara: Well, I don't know. When I play a character, I usually try to
draw on *their* background. Like when we did the Native one, I
don't really know much about them, so I tried to put in what I do
know.
KG: So what helped you?
Ciara: History classes.

I learned from our discussions that eighteen of the nineteen
girls personally identified with some aspect of the created story
in order to build the characters and the world they inhabit. Generally speaking, the students of colour and the new Canadians
felt particularly strongly about including aspects of their own
lives and 'attitudes' in their process of character development,
while this seemed somewhat less significant to the white students. Almost all of the students, however, made some reference
to their feelings, or values, or understanding of 'important
issues' as guiding their work in role.

We also talked about their perceptions of the school as a
whole. I asked them whether there were other areas of the
school where they thought their personal or cultural experiences
were included or important. The responses to this question
could be divided into three categories:

1. Other classes (10 respondents).
2. No other parts of school except drama include personal/
   cultural knowledges (6 respondents).

3. Extracurricular clubs (3 respondents, all visible minorities).

The students who cited 'other classes' as including their personal or cultural knowledge noted art, English, history, religion, and music as the subjects where this is most likely to happen. Michelle said:

> Ah, yeah, like say you're doing a project in history or geography ... you need to think about your cultural background. Oh, we did a project in religion of our cultural background. So, not so much sciences and maths, but maybe languages and humanities.

Ciara offered:

> Yeah. History class. Like my grandparents are Italian and my grandfather fought in World War II. I can really ... Like, I know about the battles, 'cause my grandfather told me.

Keisha explained:

> Keisha: Yeah. In Music.
> KG: In what way?
> Keisha: What? ... Music is so spiritual and, I don't know, I just ... You can, I mean, you put your whole life into music and you can really express yourself. Writing, playing ... like, I play piano. And sometimes it just feels so good when you learn a piece and you're doing it ... you just feel so good. You're nervous but once you're finished ... (smiles)

Six students claimed that in no other part of school did they feel that their personal or cultural knowledge was called upon or validated. Jasmine explains:

> Jasmine: No, like my other classes aren't very creative.
> KG: So do you think there's a link between creativity and using your own personal experiences in your learning?
> Jasmine: Yeah

KG: Do you think personal knowledge is different from book knowledge?

Jasmine: Yeah. To me, personal knowledge is ... is like street sense and things you pick up. Like, dictionary words might help here and there ... but ...

KG: Do you think that kind of knowledge is used or accepted in schools?

Jasmine: Yeah, but not that much.

Nelumka's response was very interesting to me because she seemed to be referring to what is often cited as a 'problem' by staff in the school:

Nelumka: Like this school in general, I find that there are certain groups and it's, like, more segregated. You work together, but it's like more segregated.

KG: What do you mean by segregated?

Nelumka: Like at lunch, you see ... you can tell what ethnic group people are when you walk through the caf.

KG: Right. And is that different or the same in drama class?

Nelumka: It's different in drama class, like, sort of it's more mixed ... groups are more mixed. Your friends are everyone in drama 'cause you're acting. You're having fun. You forget about that, you know. In other classes you have to listen hard.

KG: You don't have to listen hard in drama?

Nelumka: No, no. Like in drama it's different 'cause I don't really think of it as like a class. It's more like an extracurricular thing for me.

KG: Really?

Nelumka: It's like, you still have to work for it, but it's not like forced work.

Tenisha and Schantel, both Afro-Canadian, cited their multicultural, extracurricular group as the place in the school that most includes all aspects of who they are. They offered responses that highlight other significant advantages these groups of racial or ethnic affiliation can offer them:

Tenisha: Like a club?

KG: Yeah.

Tenisha: Well I think the 'Sisters of United Colour.'

KG: In what way?

Tenisha: I think it helps ... Like this year it helped me a lot, like talk to people one on one ... like Mrs. Waller ... like my personal problems and stuff. Like, you can't do that in a class. Like there's some teachers you can talk to but not really in a class.

I should include here that six years previously (before these girls were in the school), I acted as the moderator of the club, known as 'Africa's Own,' because there were no teachers of colour in the school and the club was in danger of being disbanded because they could not find a moderator. For two years, I worked with students on such large-scale projects as 'Black History Awareness Night.' When an Afro-Caribbean teacher was hired, she became the moderator of this group, which is now known as 'Sisters of United Colour.'

Schantel articulated clearly the service she feels her 'club' is providing her:

Schantel: Oh yeah, like mostly they [clubs] talk about different out-of-school things you can do to help you get along in school, since it is harder ... I believe it is harder for us to learn.

KG: When you say 'us,' who do you mean?

Schantel: African-Canadians. We don't feel as if we can accomplish as much. The group helps us pull ourselves back.

KG: Do you think there are other things that help you 'pull yourselves back,' besides yourselves?

Schantel: No not really. I guess like other peers maybe. There's not really like Black teachers in the school, well only one, and that would help also. And it's now 'Sisters of United Colour,' so it's not only Black people, it's Spanish ... so it's for everybody.

One might hypothesize that the basic curriculum in schools does not sufficiently include representations and voices of people of colour. Our conversations clearly point to further research

possibilities to investigate why this question generated responses that divide quite strongly along racial lines.

Next, I invited the students to reflect on their single-sex context: '*Do you think being in a classroom of all girls makes a difference in how you work in class?*' To this question, all nineteen participants answered strongly in the affirmative. They also responded with a great deal of authority on the subject, despite, in most cases, never having had a co-educational experience at the high-school level. The majority of girls, therefore, based their responses on previous elementary-school experiences of co-education. In considering why their participation is 'different' in a single-sex setting, two general themes emerged from their answers. First, the description of feeling 'more comfortable' was repeated numerous times by many students. Second, other students suggested that they would feel 'judged' and repeated words like 'intimidated,' self-conscious,' and 'stupid' in their predictions of how they would feel in a mixed class of girls and boys. Michelle stated:

Michelle: Yes! If it were co-ed, I don't think a lot of people would be as comfortable. Like in the beginning of the year when you had those name games, I think a lot of people would find those a lot more intimidating with the opposite sex or whatever.
KG: Why do you think that is?
Michelle: Um, one reason is some girls would feel they have to impress them so they ... I don't know, personally, for me I would feel more intimidated. Going to an all-girls school, it's definitely not the same. I think I learn a lot better.

Daniella referred to her memories of elementary school in her response:

Daniella: Probably. With boys I'd feel more self-conscious.
KG: Why do you think that is?
Daniella: Well in elementary school, with guys there ... they always have an opinion about what you do. Girls, like I find, are more accepting.

Christina echoed these memories of elementary school in her account:

> Christina: Yeah I would be different.
> KG: How would you be different?
> Christina: I probably wouldn't be interested as much.
> KG: Why wouldn't you?
> Christina: It's more comfortable with just girls. Well I think it's more comfortable. Well, first of all, in my elementary school, guys were always putting up their hand, always talking. And it's OK if they screw up an answer 'cause they can be just guys or whatever. Here, it's OK though.
> KG: It's OK to be wrong here?
> Christina: Yeah.

Marcella, who had attended a co-educational school in her first year of high school, offered these insights:

> Marcella: I used to go to a co-ed school and it is different. I can remember a time in grade 9 when I was so scared to say anything. You're more worried about everything, like parents ... it's just a total different environment.
> KG: What about in drama class? What if it was co-ed?
> Marcella: Yeah. Everyone would be shyer 'cause like in drama you learn the way everybody is. I know that they're like the same sex as me and it's more comfortable.

Tenisha reiterated Marcella's sense of 'comfort' in a single-sex setting and also pointed to the second emergent theme from the responses: the feeling of being 'judged.'

> Tenisha: Yeah, it would be different. I would ... at first ... I'd probably be more uncomfortable.
> KG: Why do you think that is?
> Tenisha: I don't know. Because with females, you're with your own gender. You feel more comfortable with your female friends. With guys watching? I don't know. I don't think I'd express

myself deeply. And plus, when you express yourself in drama, people learn a lot about you. I'm sure you know a lot of things about me, so I wouldn't want guys knowing, you know, things that hurt me, things that make me laugh.

KG: You feel safer with girls?

Tenisha: Yeah, I mean, I know girls talk, but they ... they ... they understand. And guys wouldn't really understand. They'd probably judge you or are more likely to judge you.

It became very apparent during these individual interviews that a sense of judgment in co-educational settings was shared by most of the girls. This sense of judgment included both their physical characteristics and their academic abilities. One girl even suggested that girls might 'hide' their intelligence:

Sandy: Yeah, if there were guys in the school I think you'd be more afraid to show that you're smarter.

KG: You'd want to hide that?

Sandy: Yeah.

KG: Why do you think that is?

Sandy: They might criticize you.

KG: So you'd feel more judged?

Sandy: Yeah.

Lily explains:

Lily: So much! With guys you have to look good for them ... fix your hair. Now I can just walk around like this (gesturing to her untucked blouse).

KG: If the Principal doesn't see you. (laughter)

Melissa felt she, too, would feel self-conscious by the mere presence of boys:

Yup. I would be more shy. You know, when you're around guys you don't feel ... you're not very comfortable with yourself. Like 'OK do I look good? Does she look better than me? Is there some-

thing wrong with me right now?' When it's an all-girls school, you have to be treated the same way.

Other students, however, seemed very concerned with how boys would significantly change their experience of school. Nancy offered:

Yes. [strongly] See, in a co-ed class, it would be like, harder for me 'cause, see like, the way we look towards boys. If I do something stupid or if I answer wrong, they'll look at me as if I'm stupid, you know. And guys put girls like they're really smart and stuff. And see over here, we don't have no one to impress, so if I think the answer's right or wrong it doesn't matter 'cause you gave it your best shot.

Graciella suggested:

Graciella: Yeah, 'cause if you're with boys you feel intimidated, you'd be more shy and it'd be harder to pay attention. And you'd be more shy to act, especially at this age, people wouldn't partici-pate and you wouldn't really get a mixture.
KG: And do you think you escape that with being with all girls?
Graciella: Yeah, like if you have a bad day, no one really looks down on you.

Finally, Keisha uniquely expressed her reasons for preferring a single-sex environment:

Keisha: Yeah. Very different.
KG: How?
Keisha: The way I think of it is, like, girls will be more hush around guys and guys like to show off around girls and they'll be more to impress girls but girls will be more down. With no guys here we're able to project a lot more. I think it's better.

After our conversations, it was clear that the girls believed they would feel less comfortable, less capable, and less in control of

their learning environment in a mixed-sex classroom. There is no doubt that girls can also judge each other harshly, but the quality of judgment that these girls are expressing underlines their fear of impotence, the uneven playing field in mixed classrooms. Although I did not, myself, attend a single-sex school as an adolescent and I did have some strong reservations about teaching in one at the beginning of my career, I have repeatedly seen evidence of the many benefits for girls when they feel more powerful, less judged, and freer to participate in their learning experiences in school. What I bring to my classrooms is a deep commitment to equity. Even single-sex classrooms are not neutral spaces. It is an explicit approach in my teaching to place equity centrally in learning and to challenge any assumptions that limit students' sense of themselves or others. These responses from my students – their own words – have confirmed many of my observations about their experiences of an all-girls drama classroom.

The 'Insider' Outside Eyes: Videographer Voices

My questionnaire was completed by the four videographers six months after the end of the taping sessions, allowing for some retrospection on the classroom activities. (At the time of the taping, the four students were in their graduating year, but their reflections on their participation in the study occurred after their graduation.) As the taping spanned two school years, the two original videographers had graduated by the second year of taping and two current (at that time) students joined the study. The four students were selected because of their interest, willingness, and availability. One of the girls is African Canadian, one is bi-racial (Afro-Caribbean and Hungarian heritage), and two are Italian Canadian. Although unintentional, this diversity in the backgrounds of the student observers was desirable. At the time of their reflections, three of the four young women had begun university programs (drama in education; women's studies; and English) and the fourth, a community college program (marketing and advertising). I asked the four young women to respond as completely as they could to the following eight questions:

1. In your role as videographer and in your observations of students' work in class, what evidence did you notice of the girls' artistic expression within the drama work?
2. In your observations, did you see evidence of cognitive responses from students in their 'working out' of problems inside the dramas?
3. If you observed evidence of a collective process in the classroom, how would you describe it?
4. Can you recall/describe any examples of personal development in the classroom as you watched students working in role?
5. Could you see evidence of girls' bringing aspects of their own lives into the work they were doing in the drama classroom?
6. What other observations did you make as an outside observer to the work the grade 10 drama students were doing in class?
7. Are there any comments you would make about your experience over an extended period of time in the drama class?
8. Did you recognize anything from the workings of the class that brought you back to your own experiences as a grade 10 drama student?

The responses to the questionnaire produced both anticipated and unanticipated outcomes. First, it was enormously helpful to gain the insights of the 'outsider' perspectives of the four senior-level students. I had anticipated that, from their particular vantage point, their observations would add to the overall understanding of our classroom context in significant ways. What was unanticipated was the extent to which the classroom work that they observed served to mediate their own perceptions of *their* experiences in a single-sex drama class at the beginning of their high-school career. Now in postsecondary education, they provided responses that offered a related but new perspective on drama and girls, for they had the benefit of their maturity and distance from their own experience of the school and their tenth-grade drama class. These 'insiders,' who were conversant with the aims of drama education yet at some distance from the actual events, provided an unanticipated but appreciated

dimension to our understanding of the context and the players by offering their own memories and reflections about the quality of their experiences in the given context.

Some of the observations of these young women seemed to echo many of my own observations, such as: students' sense of pride in their work and their ability to work as a group. Clara noted that they 'did not merely throw together a scene but instead worked intently on having it well done.' Two of the videographers, Maria and Kohlia, also described in some detail the 'collective process' or coalition-building they saw:

> There was a level of participation expected from one another when the girls were working collectively. The girls would 'brainstorm' for ideas or solutions. Once they had decided on anything, there was a period of constructive criticism. Students would make suggestions to one another even if the work was not a 'group piece.'

Kohlia explained:

> The collective process in the classroom through either small groups or the entire class, was incredibly well organized. By this I mean that the girls respected each other's ideas and comments. Because of this they were able to collectively take a situation to higher levels of thought and responses. The collective process came in many forms; discussion as a class or small group was the starting point for most of the dramas. It then went to be a process of physically developing scenes or tableaux, which is a collective in itself as all the girls had to voice an opinion and respect others. This process was incredible to watch as the students created finished works in a short period of time with great efficiency.

This student's observation was particularly interesting as I had understood the process work to be rather slow and not always leading to 'finished works.' Instead, I had noted 'efficiency' in the girls' attempts to accommodate many different contributions and ideas into the whole picture. Kohlia's further insights about the 'personal development' in the classroom,

though, corroborated my earlier descriptions of the 'collective will' to keep the drama moving. She writes:

> I cannot single out one girl who personally developed in the class, but I can recall that most girls who were shy gained self-confidence. This confidence was shown as they were much more comfortable in front of the group when doing a scene and so their voice was clearer and they were able to characterize a lot better. They also seemed to be much more willing in discussions in class about the dramas. The dramas also allowed students who were easily distracted to become focused in the group because they understood that the drama could not keep moving unless everyone was willing to participate in a positive manner.

In the questionnaire, I specifically asked the videographers to consider whether they had seen evidence that the girls included aspects of their own lives in the drama worlds they created because this had been persistently present in my observations of the classroom work and subsequently in the interviews with members of the classes. Recognizing the complexity of the question itself, I was impressed by the level at which the videographers had recalled this aspect of the work. Clara noted:

> There was also evidence of girls bringing aspects of their own lives into the work being done in class. This did not surface in the form of girls telling their intimate secrets, but instead came through their characterizations in the drama. I specifically remember seeing a number of scenes with parents speaking to their child. The portrayal of the parents was always much different because the girls portrayed these characters as though it was their own parents.

Selina offered an illuminating observation on the question of girls' using 'aspects of their own lives' by observing how the girls drew on their own cultural knowledge. She explains:

> St Jude's is a high school that is very culturally diverse. There was

one assignment in particular where students were asked to bring one item from home and explain [as the character] why the item is meaningful to them. In this case the students *literally* brought aspects of their culture and heritage into class. This however happens in every drama class in more subtle ways. The subjects discussed are often modern issues that can affect the lives of all women. Discussions were often quite passionate for this reason and the girls often participate with enthusiasm. The drama class addresses issues of racism, sexism, classism, pregnancies, and much more. The girls have in most cases experienced these subjects in their personal lives. Drama exposes these moments by re-creating them.

I am struck by Selina's observation that 'drama exposes these moments by re-creating them.' By using drama conventions, the girls had claimed these 'modern issues' that addressed their lived experiences. My classroom experience had taught me that taking 'experience' as the contextual basis of students' knowledge leads to richer learning. I was gratified when this was actually 'observable' to others.

Finally, an unanticipated but greatly appreciated outcome of the questionnaire was the videographers' recollections of their own experiences as grade 10 drama students in a single-sex setting. Two of the four focused on their memories of personal and 'group' accomplishment; one on her sense of 'inclusion' of difference and diversity; and the other on the qualities of single-sex and Catholic education.

The final open-ended question on the questionnaire asked: 'Did you recognize anything from the workings of the class that brought back to you your own experiences as a grade 10 drama student?' Maria recounted:

Through watching the students I must admit that many of my own experiences as a grade 10 student came back. The first thing I remembered was the way I felt when I had to do a scene in front of twenty-five people. But I also remembered the sense of accomplishment that I felt when we had worked out a scene or a tab-

leau. The confidence I saw growing in the students, I remember growing in myself when I was in their place.

Kohlia referred to her sense of group accomplishment:

As a graduated student, videotaping this class brought back many memories of drama class. I remember thinking of drama as an art and not immaturely like 'pretend,' stories like 'Earth-woman' and 'Nothing but the Truth.' The second story especially brought back memories because when my group did it many years before, it was one of our best pieces.

Selina also referred to a specific drama, but what stayed with her was the question that had been most important to her at the time:

Although each class is very different, the material covered and the friendly atmosphere remain the same. The story of a human woman and the star [husband] brought back many memories of the class I was in. This brought to the surface issues of bi-racial children and ended in a heated conflict. One aspect that remains the same is that no matter what race, class, or ethnicity you are from you are able to voice your opinion and it is just as valuable as anyone else's.

Clara goes into some detail, using her current understanding of the world to filter her memories of her experiences in a single-sex, Catholic institution. She explains:

It is interesting as a former St Jude's student and now a women's studies major, re-evaluating my own experience in the all-female drama program. I now believe that every student is confronted with questions that they may not be aware of until after the program is completed: (1) What is a woman composed of? (2) What am I composed of? These are the two questions that I have been focusing on for years. It was the experience of being able to participate in an all-female drama class that has influenced me greatly.

All of these years I have been on a 'voyage' in finding myself. The drama program allowed me to see parts of myself that I never knew existed. I was faced with developing myself as a woman. Observing these students brought back many memories for me as a grade 10 student. For one, being a grade 10 student in an all-female and Catholic school is extremely oppressive. It is not being in an all-female institution that is oppressive. It is the pressure of the religion itself, that would like 'mould' every female student into the 'ideal patriarchal woman.' These students that are lucky enough to participate in an all-female drama program have the opportunity to see beyond and above the institution. If these students take this new experience and use it to develop themselves, they will be able to answer these questions and find out how influential this all-female program is.

The striking observations and insights and the stirring personal recollections of the videographers do more than simply include the differently positioned voices of these observers. In my view, the articulation of their experiences as 'insider outside eyes' to the work enlarges our understanding of the complexities of adolescent female development and indicates many other avenues for exploration, such as girls' social and personal development and the place the arts may occupy at critical points in that process.

Becoming a Teacher-Researcher

By doing teacher research in the classroom, we take on the role (students and teacher together) of inquisitors. Being inquisitors puts teachers and students in a powerful position. Freire (1998b, 66) believed that our capacity to learn is the source of our ability to teach. Good 'lessons' may help us navigate, but it is probing questions that enrich our practice. I did not set out, for example, to determine how girls can improve their self-esteem, but I was interested in understanding what was present in the classroom when girls' self-esteem was intact. That is the stance of the reflective practitioner.

As I collected data, I was hoping to better understand the particular qualities of drama education for girls in a single-sex environment. I was looking for more than a glimpse at the often ephemeral moments in an arts class. I wanted to capture every aspect of the classroom action by videotaping the daily workings of five drama classes over two years to observe the quality and form of their experiences in drama.

Tomkins, Connolly, and Bernier (1981) argue that the field of curriculum studies reflects the complex, action-oriented, situation-specific character of particular phenomena in educational contexts. One of the principal ways, they suggest, of having impact in educational practice is to have research follow, rather than precede, curriculum development. One way in which this can occur is to use the reflective-practitioner research model, of which my work is one example. It offers to educational research a particular model (that seems to be gaining considerable momentum) of participant observation in which the teacher becomes researcher. My study was especially interested in bringing the classroom and the teacher more fully into the research picture. This story of research began with looking at girls and inevitably ended with looking at myself looking at the girls.

The real strength of this approach is its attention to the contextualized voices and setting of each classroom. What I have offered here about questions of equity in education and insights into drama education is firmly grounded in a particular context and will illuminate theory that emerges from evidence rather than theory that is superimposed on evidence. Ineluctably, researchers bring themselves to the data and operate from a particular stance. Wolcott (1990) claims that he personalizes the world he researches and intellectualizes the one he experiences; in short, one does not need to be neutral in order to be objective. In my systematic and extensive study of drama education in a single-sex school for girls, I aimed, ultimately, to offer convincing insights into the art of classroom drama and the girls who make it.

Assumptions and Paradigms: Three Propositions to Consider

1. Teacher-researchers investigate the questions that inform and animate their practice.

All research endeavours, whether qualitative or quantitative, reflect a paradigm, a world-view or set of propositions, that explains how the world is perceived by the researcher. Hawthorne (1992, 126) states that a paradigm is composed of 'a set of beliefs that both enables and constrains research: a framework or scaffold, which can underpin or support further work but which, of necessity, also excludes a range of possibilities.' In short, the conceptual framework of a researcher directs our attention in particular ways, and, as Eisner (1991) concludes, what we experience is shaped by that framework.

The teacher-researcher, driven by the questions of a daily practice, makes the theory/practice dichotomy less one of polarities and more one of an active and reflexive relationship. Eisner (1971) warned that the relationship of scientific theory to practice in the field of curriculum is, as in other fields, a tenuous one at best. Kaufmann (1971), examining curriculum-making in the arts, operates from the supposition that the act of teaching is an unfinished event until the actual teacher, children, particular situation, and environment are in active relationship. As a corollary to this, teacher-researchers might consider the 'research event' unfinished until the local concerns and needs of the students are brought to bear on the practices and therefore the reflecting-on-practices, or theorizing, of the teacher. It is these three dimensions – the students, the context, and the teacher practices – that must fuel research in curriculum.

Teacher-researcher studies are context-dependent and, some might argue, less easily generalizable; but they are, to a great degree, important for initiating theory construction. An in-depth study of a particular setting can offer descriptions and interpretations that go beyond that specific setting. The benefits of classroom-based research can be contextualized and understood

because of, rather than in spite of, its specific nature. It will, however, demand work from its readers, asking them to reflect back to their own contexts. Pieces of a particular context are often illuminated when seen at a critical distance; rather than replicating laboratory experiments and preserving variables from one context to another, the particular and unique qualities of one qualitative study might illuminate the particular elements of another.

In the case of my classes, for instance, the many subjectivities from which young women speak and act became clear. When gender is 'relaxed,' other categories of identity are often fore-grounded. As I have illustrated with girls' stories in Chapter 2, 'difference' rather than 'sameness' becomes magnified in a sin-gle-sex setting. This kind of heightened reality will have impli-cations for other environments, including co-educational ones. Eisner (1991) reminds us that all learning involves generaliza-tion, that is, a person's ability to display or understand what has been learned in a new situation. Since no two situations are identical, generalization must occur.

2. *Educational research is a collaborative conversation about learning that involves, engages, and informs both teachers and learners.*

The word curriculum comes from the Latin *currere*, meaning 'to run,' as in running a course. 'To run' suggests a span – progress – moving forward. Not surprisingly, then, Stenhouse (1975) claims that curriculum allows teachers and students to test things; that the medium of the classroom action is curriculum. As a drama practitioner and a teacher-researcher, I am attracted to these definitions and descriptions of curriculum for they sug-gest the movement that is at the centre of inquiry-based curric-ula and the necessary interaction between teacher and learner that takes place.

In my experience, learning in a group and committing to a group project often lead to a kind of coalition-building among different groups in a classroom. I believe that taking 'experience' as the contextual basis of students' knowledge leads to richer

learning. But 'perspectivism' (Eisner, 1991) is not an attractive idea to those who believe there is one way to see a problem or one experience to turn to as a representative experience.

3. *The arts are a valuable way of merging the individual with the whole.*

In the field of social sciences, Burrell and Morgan (1979) clearly explicate the perennial debate between determinism and voluntarism, suggesting that the assumptions of many social scientists are pitched somewhere in between. In the field of developmental psychology (Isaacs, 1993; Winnicott, 1971; Piaget and Inhelder, 1975), considerable research confirms the existence of make-believe and inquiry in the young child and the impetus to challenge and change in the adolescent. In fact, adolescents, like no other group, quite willingly commit themselves to possibilities. They not only try to adapt their egos to the social environment, but, just as emphatically, try to adjust the environment to their egos (Piaget and Inhelder, 1975).

Philosophers (Wilshire, 1991) and drama educators (Courtney, 1989; O'Neill, 1995) alike have argued that drama puts us in touch with things that are too far or too close to see in our ordinary 'offstage' life; that we are deeply affected by the fictions we enact in this communal act of imagination. In fact, students often grasp the actual through the fictional when their world becomes mapped into the 'world' they are creating. The experience of doing drama calls on the 'inner and private' to work with 'the outer and public' parts of ourselves and leaves open, as Wilshire (1991) says, the tension of the universal and the particular.

Finally, Freire (1998b) points to our social relations in his celebration of the democratic and emancipatory imperatives of education. He says:

Our being is a *being with*. So, to be in the world without making history, without being made by it, without creating culture, without a sensibility towards one's own presence in the world, without a dream, without song, music, or painting, without caring for

the earth or the water, without using one's hands, without sculpting or philosophizing, without any opinion about the world, without doing science or theology, without awe in the face of mystery, without learning, instruction, teaching, without ideas on education, without being political, is a total impossibility. (58)

The Importance of Evaluating the Arts in Schools

'I would like to think that in the 21st century, people will be able to achieve fulfilment more from being and doing than from getting and having. One of the implications of this would be much greater attention to the arts' (Pratt, 1987, 623). In his paper, Pratt is looking for curriculum options for the twenty-first century and is reminding us that life is vast and mysterious. Why would we only prepare for one cramped corner of it? If education does not offer students aesthetic experiences, then it is in danger of depriving them of the essential means of fulfilment beyond careers and acquisitions. It is the responsibility of schools to prepare students for the richness of living, and one way to do this is to include aesthetic experiences in their learning, without which they will surely have impoverished images of human progress.

The patterns of educational reform in the latter years of the twentieth century have evolved from the deficit discourse of neoconservative governments. In an effort to re-evaluate spending in education, governments talk a good deal about 'paring down,' 'cutting the fat,' rather than opening up; about reinforcing rather than reinventing. 'Art for art's sake' has fallen out of favour, but Kaufmann (1971) pointed out that 'art for art's sake' is really 'art for people's sake.' A rationale for arts education, a position of defence, would not be necessary if Maxine Greene's (1978) proposition – that the primary purpose of education is to foster a multi-perspectival view of life – were taken seriously. At the turning of the millennium, as directions for curriculum reform are contemplated, the arts have a significant role to play.

For example, drama is often more concerned about a 'process' than a 'product,' although it may result in very fine products. It

is possible to assess a process, but the wrong kind of assessment can halt a process and arrest its movement. Students often see assessment as a final judgment, something that congeals the movement of a process and brings a kind of stasis to the experience. Arts educators, therefore, must struggle with the assessment of artistic processes, given the current trend toward measurable, quantifiable, 'testable' educational outcomes. This would mean a greater reliance on holistic scoring instruments.

A teacher might begin a course, for instance, by asking students to perform an initial assessment of themselves. Following the scale A–Always, O–Often, S–Sometimes, R–Rarely, and N–Never, I would have students check the appropriate level for each of the following statements:

During drama, I:
Listen carefully to instructions
Work seriously
Have care and concern for others
Am willing to do things I haven't done before
Work effectively through problems
Understand the purpose of the activities
Can think, write, and talk about the significance of the activities

In addition to this, two final questions – 'Comment on those things you enjoy doing in drama' and 'Comment on those things you don't enjoy or find difficult' – provide some initial qualitative data about the student's response to drama. In an attempt to move away from evaluation as a final judgment, it is important to understand a student's orientation to the subject right from the start.

Following a process drama, in which students would be involved in role-playing and improvisational activities, I would suggest a similar scale (A, O, S, R, N) for holistic assessment of each student's work:

The student:
• Adopts and sustains appropriate roles in drama

- Demonstrates an awareness of the dramatic situation and con- tributes positively to its development
- Responds in-role with appropriate verbal behaviour
- Responds in-role with appropriate nonverbal behaviour
- Initiates ideas for the group both in and out of role
- Demonstrates an awareness of and a sensitivity to what is being created in the improvisational work
- Reflects on the drama, verbally and in writing, in ways that demonstrate an understanding of its significance

To this I would add my anecdotal comments that would further ground my assessments in classroom observations. Following the process drama work, the student, too, would be asked to evaluate herself on each of the above criteria, adding any further observations about her learning process that she might have made. These are the kinds of ongoing assessments that need to be made in the drama classroom in order to respect the fluid nature of thinking and learning through the arts. It is an explicit assumption of my work that the arts are necessary. Following from this, it is equally fundamental to retain an assessment of process drama that does not halt that process but takes account of the essential movement that lies at its centre. This is why research in the arts is crucial, particularly research carried out by teachers in classrooms who work in these modes that challenge positivist assertions about educational research and evaluation.

Often case studies of classrooms (Taylor, 1996; Hundert, 1996; Edmiston and Wilhelm, 1996) highlight episodes that reveal the participants' own words. Feagin et al. (1991) have perhaps sum- marized best this kind of work in the following description:

> The qualitative research exemplified in the case study brings us closer to real human beings and everyday life. Rather than assum- ing a world of simplicity and uniformity, those who adopt the qual- itative approach picture a world of complexity and plurality. (23)

My teacher research operated from a conceptual orientation that uses qualitative inquiry both to see and to make sense of

what has been seen (Eisner, 1991). It is what Madeleine Grumet (1989) has called a 'picture of the seeing' (87). In my multi-case study, I drew on ethnography and reflective-practitioner methods to pose questions and gain insight into the kind and quality of experiences my students were having. In individual interviews, in whole-class discussions, in personal and group writing-in-role, and in personal written reflection, I listened closely to the explanations of their choices and actions in the classroom and their involvements in the imagined worlds we built.

Chapter Four

Teacher Roles and the Curriculum

But is achieving excellence in teaching a realistic aim? It seems to me that the reality is an aspiration, and that aspiration to excellence is a reality. Excellence still exists, and it always did. But the conditions that promote excellence rarely exist, and they rarely have. So we have a choice, whether in conditions that often scarcely contribute to excellence, to choose to aspire to it. We can practise choosing; we can renew and review our choices. We make our choices on excellence daily, minute by minute, each choice dictating the next. You cannot reach excellence for a whole day; you can only reach it minute by minute. And this is one of the excitements of teaching – the constant exhilaration of recognizing the choices we have made at any moment. When we stop choosing, things go radically wrong with us.

If I could give young teachers anything, I would give them the ability to negotiate with significance. This, to me, is what high quality endeavour means.
Dorothy Heathcote, Excellence in Teaching (1984)

The Drama Practitioner: Imagining Possibilities

Gavin Bolton (1984) uses the term 'loving ally' when discussing the function of teachers (34). This certainly reflects the shift from the concept of teacher as disseminator of knowledge to a kind of child-centredness at the heart of the teacher's work. It is also clearly about the child's relationship to the world. If we are interested in an approach that places the child in the centre of our work with them, then we must begin by acknowledging cer-

tain fundamental things about the world we live in and the institutions we teach in.

Kathleen Weiler (1988), in her studies of gender, class, and power in education, asks teachers to acknowledge their own assumptions and the assumptions of the dominant ideology whose interests are served by the institutions in which they teach. Weiler's critical pedagogy is about the relations that teachers and students enter into as part of the process of production and exchange around specific forms of knowledge and values, and the cultural practices such relations support with respect to dominant or emancipatory interests. She asks us to acknowledge that disempowerment is built into the system. In other words, we must acknowledge that to be productive between and through all the varying categories of race, class, and gender, our roles need to be active and changeable.

This thinking leads me to a broader understanding of what it means to teach that still contains within it a concrete idea about the 'role' of teacher: the person in the equation who creates the spaces of possibility, who does not find solutions but nurtures the questions, while asking the learners to bring what they already know to bear on what they are learning. This means, as Starratt (1990) would have it, that an 'awareness of the possibilities in every learning opportunity is awareness of the intrinsic drama of schooling, for every learning opportunity is about issues in growth or defeat – no matter how small' (105).

The role of the teacher of drama is magnified, as both teachers and students are 'senders' and 'receivers' in *and* out of role. Pioneer drama teacher Dorothy Heathcote (in Johnson and O'Neill, 1984) found that the most secure authority – the authority of role – has always been found within the drama situation rather than the teaching situation. This is possibly because drama teachers, as part of their craft, must know how to 'give up' power in role, to direct the drama from various registers within the context of the group. Drama teachers must often 'feel' when to move in and when to move out. The striking of this careful balance is often more easily executed if the teacher is seen to be 'in role' (in solidarity, in cahoots, in the game) with the students.

At times, however, this can be a precarious place for teachers. Being both inside and outside the work is a demanding requirement. It means that teachers do not forget their 'teacher self' but often allow students to believe they have done so. I maintain that reflection is at the heart of effective teaching. Teachers, then, while participating in the narrative-building, must not relinquish the role of leader in a collective learning space. This means that, as leaders, we must be involved enough to feel the momentum of the work, but detached enough to formulate questions and conduct action.

In this way teachers must also look very closely at error. In errors we can see clearly where choices may have ceased to create possibilities for learning. Likewise, it is necessary to look at those 'lessons' or collaborative experiences that seemed to work especially well with students to determine which ingredients invited learning. Because teachers and students of drama are deeply involved in a process way of being, it is essential that teachers have the time to reflect seriously about that process. Wells and Chang-Wells (1992) suggest that in a community of inquirers, the roles of teacher and learner are interchangeable, for 'all are learning and, at the same time, helping others to learn' (51). A burden may be lifted from teachers if we successfully shift paradigms and begin to see ourselves inside this learning process, players in the game instead of controllers of its outcomes.

Bringing the World In

Teachers interested in transforming education must start with the student culture. Clar Doyle (1993) claims that we must give experience a stronger place in education, and states that who is learning precedes what is learned. This seems a logical conclusion to draw, yet so much of our organization around teaching ignores and even denies that our students come to us with a wealth of knowledge and experiences that have already shaped them. But teachers should not simply concern themselves with exploring the problems or issues of the students. They must hear these problems so that students might themselves pose new

questions about their worlds. It is a process of both knowing what we know and doubting what we know. When teachers are reflective about their work with students, it often follows that students, too, become more reflective about their concerns.

Gavin Bolton (1971) suggested that we have moved from the concept of 'good teachers' in drama to a child-centred philosophy in drama. Ironically perhaps, this approach necessarily demands even better teachers, teachers whose skills are more refined, whose sense of their place in the whole picture is more clear, and who find ways to engage the lives of their students without abdicating their responsibility to structure the learning. David Best (1985) describes it in this way:

> A work of art, and through it a perceptive teacher or critic, can reveal the character of sincere feelings, and give the possibility of deeper and more finely discriminated emotional experiences. (194)

In drama education, we might be more accurate if we were to call drama work not 'works of art' but 'workings of art.' Consciously relating the learning of something to its effect on human living is a critical part of the work of a reflective teacher. Teachers of drama, then, must be especially attentive to the unique qualities of their contexts. In this way, the social worlds their students imagine become the substance, the textbook, of the lesson; to these worlds students bring their interests and experiences.

Drama teachers must also have the opportunity to redo, rerun, or improve a lesson. Just as we always afford students the possibility of slowing down the work, rehearsing, or changing their minds, so too must we be as flexible with ourselves. Students must know that we do not always make the best choices the first time around and that it is profitable to revisit old places. In this way, the learning can be seen as genuinely process-driven for both students and teacher. Dorothy Heathcote (1984c) summarizes this idea well:

> If we are to give more than lip service to creativity in children, we

must actively support the creativity of the teacher. That is to say, we must come to recognize fully the creativity of good teaching. (79)

Finally, teachers ought to be passionate about more than their teaching. They will then bring their passions and their commitments to their teaching, and infuse their work with the creativity of their whole lives. When teachers acknowledge their 'roles' in the 'dramas' outside the classroom, they are allowing the learning experiences within schools to move beyond the walls of the schools. As much as we would not want a classroom of dutiful students, nor should they want a dutiful teacher whose 'real' life is left behind, whose interests are left disengaged.

It was just before the Remembrance Day presentation of 1994, described in the beginning of this book, that I returned to my classroom after living through the final two weeks of my father's battle with cancer. In his last moments, we listened to the beautiful renditions of war tunes by John McDermott, a transplanted Scot like my father. As we were listening to the last stanza of the air 'By Yon Bonny Banks' – a song written in 1746 and based on an old Celtic belief that when a man dies in a foreign land, his spirit returns via the low road – my father slipped away. I returned to my classroom changed, as we are all changed by our personal experiences, and I became a different teacher. Like our students, we are not invulnerable; we do not operate from compartments, but are whole people, each day reconciling all of who we are with what we do. Freire (1998b) insisted on the principle that although teachers and students are different, the teacher is being formed or re-formed as he or she teaches, and the person who is being taught forms himself or herself in the process. He describes:

When we live our lives with the authenticity demanded by the practice of teaching that is also learning and learning that is also teaching, we are participating in a total experience that is simultaneously directive, political, ideological, gnostic, pedagogical, aesthetic, and ethical. In this experience the beautiful, the decent, and the serious form a circle with hands joined. (31–2)

Like us, our students experience risk when we let them reflect on their lives, find their meanings, and create their 'selves.' But with this risk and through the abstraction of role in drama, students have a unique opportunity to better understand their world and each other. Booth and Thornley-Hall (1991) explain the power of role-play in the following way:

> Role lets children leave the narrow confines of their own worlds and gives them entry into new forms of existence. At the same time, they must find a sense of their own relationships to this fictional life, the 'me in the role' and the 'role in me.' When children participate in drama, they are in charge of building the dramatic experience through their actions and words. They become the drama, discovering ideas and directions that will surprise and change them. Because meanings are being made and not given, the children will find responses and language powers that are unexpected, engendered by the collective drive for group meaning. (95)

The teacher must be prepared to allow students to find the 'role in them' and to arrive at some surprising places. Of course, drama does not always succeed in inviting students to engage their lives in their work and to construct new knowledge, but the chances of engaging the students in a meaningful experience that has the potential of transforming their thinking is increased if the teacher is able to create the task that will focus their questioning. Wells and Chang-Wells (1992) suggest that learning should always be undertaken in the context of a meaningful activity, and that the 'significance of the component parts be understood in relation to the achievement of the goal of the activity as a whole' (29). In role, students create worlds within which they find voices and language, silence and movement, to represent their questions and engage their problems. The 'tasks' in drama, created by thoughtful and imaginative teachers, provide the frame for their personal exploration within the group. This kind of structure invites students' lives into the classroom so they can begin to reflect on the ways their learning might bring new light to bear on their lives beyond the classroom walls.

The Action of Curriculum: When Objectives Meet Practice

Curriculum is a moving form. That is why we have trouble capturing it, fixing it in language, lodging it in our matrix. Whether we talk about it as history, as syllabi, as classroom discourse, as intended learning outcomes, or as experience, we are trying to grasp a moving form, to catch it at the moment that it slides from being the figure, the object and goal of action, and collapses into the ground of action.

Madeleine Grumet, *Bitter Milk: Women and Teaching* (1988)

There is a rich body of literature in drama education written by both drama educators/researchers and theorists who acknowledge the role drama and experiential learning can play in a vital school curriculum. Students working in drama are in a process of discovering how reality is constructed. In role, they become creators of worlds. These 'worlds' run parallel to our external world, or, as Courtney (1990) would say, are the 'double' (31) of our world and aim at reconciling our inner world with the environment. He suggests:

> In order to understand other people, we 'put ourselves in their shoes' – attempt to see things from their point of view. In the drama created by our inner world, the protagonist is our Self. Other people become, in this drama, the antagonist and the chorus.' (1980, 7)

By creating a fictional drama, students are actually constructing the purposes of their learning. This is the unique and necessary contribution the drama curriculum makes to the secondary-school curriculum.

One of Dewey's (1938) central questions, emerging from a sound philosophy of experience, is how the past can engage students in the present. In constructing a parallel world, students recall the past, negotiate the present, and insinuate a future. Illuminating connections can also be made with Dewey's (1926) maxim 'An ounce of experience is better than a ton of theory' (169). It is only in experience that any theory has vital and verifiable significance. According to Dewey (1926),

To 'learn from experience' is to make a backward and forward connection between what we do to things and what we enjoy or suffer from things in consequence. Under such conditions, doing becomes a trying; an experiment with the world to find out what it is like; the undergoing becomes instruction – discovery of the connections of things. (164)

Drama education is a practice that demands of the student an understanding of lived past experiences in order to inform the present. This is what Courtney (1990) has called the actual world informing the fictional world and, in turn, the fictional world inspiring the actual world, for 'they are not separate cognitive categories' (18). They complement each other and share common properties.

Cameron Ross (1988), in his analysis of Dorothy Heathcote's work, explains that Heathcote radically changed the way educational drama was conceptualized: 'Drama arises from socially negotiated and constructed contexts – teacher as meaning-maker, who with children, attended to the world evoked through the art form' (41). Bolton (1984) suggests that drama entails the co-construction of meaning through collaborative student–student, student–teacher, and student–curriculum relationships. In *Re-Play: Studies of Human Drama in Education*, Courtney (1982) described drama as the active bridge between our inner world and the environment:

In drama, we re-present ourselves in the environment symbolically. Then our performance mediates between the self and the environment. We do this in order to create meaning – to understand experience and re-interpret it in ways that are meaningful to us ... In such a way, dramatic learning is highly effective, mingling cognition and feeling into a whole experience that deeply touches the self. (6)

All of these definitions identify the notion of the construction of a drama curriculum, a collaborative process that draws on students' and teachers' emotional and intellectual worlds. These

definitions also begin to suggest the inherent challenges of pre-determining educational objectives for a drama curriculum.

The Problem of Goal-Setting in the Arts

Some analysis is needed before we undertake a real probing of the educational objectives of the dramatic arts. Arts educators have traditionally resisted what they often see as an administrative imposition of educational 'aims' on their subject discipline. This is not because arts teachers want to be less accountable than other teachers, but because they frequently have serious questions about the role of goal-setting in the arts. It is possibly a more onerous task because of the nature of the more global and less easily defined goals of an arts curriculum. In addition, curriculum policymakers have not traditionally valued what might be called 'emotional learning' in schools. Far too many drama educators, therefore, are aware that outcome data are not always a measure of a program's success. Nagy (1993) describes the tension in this way:

> Decision-makers typically require outcome data as evidence of program success, while drama educators value process and often express concern about the appropriateness of outcome data for the evaluation of drama programs in education. (118)

I see three main problems for drama educators in relation to goal-setting. First, and simply put, a word like *objective* is not a neutral word but an ideologically loaded one. It implies a kind of functionalism in education that is often at odds with the more unpredictable nature of outcomes in the arts. In other words, drama educators are reluctant to overstate the place of formal 'objectives' in their program design. I suggest, here, two alternative words, which also have their own problems but which possibly better capture the idea of Dewey's 'end in view.' The first is *vision*, which, while more accurately defining the instructional stance of a drama teacher, suffers from a vagueness that further convolutes the serious and cognitive value of work in the arts.

The second is *pursuit*, which has also been devalued by its association with 'pursuits of leisure.' Alternatively, educational pursuit may have in it a measure of artistic freedom while retaining a strong sense of an 'end in view.' I have followed this avenue not because I see the rhetoric as useful in itself, but because in attempting to more accurately account for the practice of arts educators, it may be possible to bridge the seemingly large gap between curriculum designers and classroom professionals.

The second problem stems from a belief that providing experiences and training for their intrinsic value alone is itself an acceptable goal. In other words, any drama teacher knows that there is far more learning in a curriculum moment than can be categorized in the limiting objectives that can be set out.

The third and most significant problem is the way in which objectives have been drawn up in government and school district documents: they are elusive in meaning and do not easily translate into observable events. Educational drama objectives, therefore, need much further delineation in order to be useful and observable to the practitioner.

The new Ministry of Education (1999) arts curriculum documents for the province of Ontario emphasize the *theory, creation,* and *analysis* of drama as the areas in which students must demonstrate competence. While assessing students' grasp of relevant dramatic theory or analysing live productions of theatre is simpler to accomplish, it is students' competence in 'making drama' that remains more difficult to assess. These documents, driven by political accountability, require that teachers understand (and demonstrate) how well they are doing what they are doing. It is worth struggling with this question as drama teachers because there is simply so much going on that is worth doing.

In my classroom, I arrived at a general objective that helped to guide me in my understanding of how students actually work 'in role' and how they move through a dramatic process of creating: *In improvised dramatic role-play, students will begin to understand how realities are constructed.* But what does this general objective mean in specific terms? Contrary to what many believe, learning for students in drama does not occur when the

players slip deeper inside the characters they are representing. Students understand 'character' by making decisions and choices in view of the others in the created world. Therefore, it is not from moving deeper inside character that they learn about that character. Rather, the interior life of the character is manifest because of other people and the social reality they are creating. What this means in a classroom is that students will have the ability to make decisions based on their (fictional) positions of power in relation to the 'other.' This means that the students will understand the full implications of their social reality and can then demonstrate an ability to make a decision from a full awareness of their position in the fictional world. Therefore, students will know how to *make choices based on their clearly understood relationships to other people.* The teacher can now more easily go about setting up scenarios in which students will need to understand their specific relationship to others and make choices in the drama based on that understanding.

All documents aiming to evaluate the performances of drama state that students should practise and master communication skills. But what skills? and how? For clarity's sake, this objective needs to be broken down further. While engaged in drama, students have access to two levels of communication: verbal and nonverbal. By doing either, students will already have demonstrated substantial self-confidence regardless of their subsequent success at communicating. Furthermore, the student will also have already demonstrated an ability to either listen to others or observe their nonverbal or body language before entering into a communication. Here we arrive at the specific learned skill of students engaged in a drama. The students will: *(1) listen to and observe the communication of another; and (2) enter into a scene using the appropriate level of language given the socially constructed reality and/or display the well-chosen body language given their relationship to others.*

These are two easily recognizable skills the student can apply and the teacher might assess. These particular skills would again be techniques students will need to apply elsewhere in the school and certainly in the workplace.

Most Ontario school districts suggest that the secondary curriculum must 'stimulate a sense of inquiry and a commitment to life-long learning' (see Metropolitan Separate School Board, Dramatic Arts Core Curriculum, 1989). The first part of this objective – 'stimulate a sense of inquiry' – can be observed rather easily by teachers by looking carefully at their students in a role-play. Teachers realize the students are involved in a process in their 'reality-making' that involves as much how they think as what they think. It is also the quality of the movement of that thinking that is the concern of both teacher and students. Courtney (1990) explains:

> The impact of dramatic activity on the cognition processes involved in problem solving is strong because drama is always directed to a specific practice: the need to keep the action moving forward. (29)

When students make choices to 'drive a scene' we can say they are illustrating a sense of inquiry. Students are said to have inquiring minds when they *introduce a new or previously unknown or untold piece of information that has the effect of driving the scene forward.*

The second part of this objective is a far more difficult, and perhaps impossible, goal. It is truly what we might call a vision of education, an 'end in view.' To stimulate a 'commitment to life-long learning' can only be measured over a lifetime. But because it is not a negligible goal, teachers must do their best to map it onto their practice at every level. Perhaps the best that teachers of dramatic arts can do is invite students to conceive of possibility. In order to do this, they must work in the imaginative mode, and 'the fiction allows us to live through an alternative to rigid attitudes, giving us a world of dramatic possibility. The more we do so, the more intelligence becomes a factor in our lives' (Courtney, 1990, 20). I believe this might be what Pitman (1998, 249) means when he concludes that a commitment to the concept of 'lifelong learning for creativity' is an essential strategy for change in our schools. Therefore, the students will *call on*

their intelligence in tackling the problems they face in the classroom and beyond. If education becomes an important choice in their lives, we might presume that students will become life-long learners and assume their prominent place in the building of a future.

Many government and school district curriculum documents neglect one of the major components of drama education: the experience of the aesthetic and the development of artistic 'voice' or expression. By the senior years of drama, students are not only making choices about the content of dramas, they are also making artistic choices about form. They can demonstrate an understanding of the effect of dramatic form and make artistic choices that show an understanding of theatre conventions and forms. Therefore, I would also include the following objective: the student of drama will *illustrate an understanding of form by making choices about artistic representation in a dramatic mode.*

Finally, what is often left out in the assessment tools of other subject disciplines but remains an essential part of the creative assessment of the arts is what Pitman (1998) has deemed the highest level of assessment: self-examination. This form of assessment involves both student and teacher and is used regularly in most arts classes. Pitman explains that 'process folios' document the stages in the development of any project, as do journals, which students use to express their own understandings of the learning journey. To my list of objectives, then, I have added that students will *become comfortable with self-evaluation and begin to assess with discernment their own actions and thoughts within a creative process.*

To summarize, the new and clarified list of educational pursuits I would propose and deem 'measurable' are as follows:

Drama Objectives

1. Students will begin to understand how realities are constructed by:
    a) making choices based on their clearly understood relationship to other people;

    b) listening to and observing the communication of others;

    c) entering into a scene using the appropriate level of language; and/or displaying the well-chosen body language given their relationship to others;

    d) introducing a new or previously unknown or untold piece of information that has the effect of driving the scene forward;

    e) calling on their intelligence in tackling the problems they face in the classroom and beyond.

2. Students will illustrate an understanding of form by making choices about artistic representation in a dramatic mode.

3. Students will become comfortable with self-evaluation and begin to assess with discernment their own actions and thoughts within a creative process.

The Projects of Drama Are the Projects of Life

It is always a challenge for arts educators to engage with the philosophical and pedagogical questions of 'objectives' and 'aims.' In my view, the goals of all arts curricula must reflect those artistic qualities we need to live progressively in our social world. Understanding relationships, forging ahead, and working in the human community are all essential life skills. Appreciation of the arts, creative intelligence, and problem-solving skills are all valuable by-products of an arts curriculum. The projects of drama are the projects of life. It is for this reason that the *how* of learning in drama is often privileged over the *what*. Dramatic learning is hinged on structure, not content; on how action is put together and shaped. As Courtney (1990) suggests, 'metaphorically speaking, we look through Hamlet to ourselves and all humanity' (144).

Implicit in this view of dramatic arts, therefore, is a constructivist, rather than a didactic, perspective on learning. Learners are seen as active participants in the learning process who construct meaning through personal and social experiences. Pitman (1998, 119) makes a strong case for excellence in education in the next millennium. He argues that the assessment processes found

in schools that have quality arts education programs are a more reliable test of students' accomplishments in the skills and intelligences that will count most beyond the classroom than the objective tests for language, literacy, maths, and sciences.

Many would argue that the singular goal of engaging a student's affective learning makes drama a requisite of any student's experience of school. As Junell (1974) states:

> It is curious that those branches of the federal government, which so generously dispense their largesse on a confusing array of research projects, have never enlisted the aid of the gifted dramatist to help write the curriculum for the needs of the child's emotional world. (115)

We certainly cannot deny the effects a drama program will have on students who may otherwise be involved in a more traditional and often mechanistic experience of education in the school, particularly at the secondary level. The students themselves are well able to describe the 'difference' they feel in a drama class. But drama also demands higher-order thinking, as students negotiate the construction of social realities. The goal of an emancipatory curriculum in the arts is the creation of a curriculum of discernment that will ask students to understand their particular location in a social reality and make choices that advance that reality. Elizabeth Straus, in 'Drama and Generic Skills: The Movement of Skills from the Drama Class to the Workplace' (1991), substantiates the social advantages of drama in the following way:

> As the arts become recognized for their ability to supply essential life skills, those skills considered most valuable in the workplace, then the cost of programs like drama are justifiable and actually a bargain. Not only do the programs serve two functions, learning and enjoyment, but they also operate at a cost much less than other academic subjects which attempt to serve a similar function. (231)

When Peter McLaren (1986) was teaching and researching in

an inner-city Canadian school, he was acutely aware of the role of a liberating curriculum in the lives of his students. Drama, for him, was one method by which educators could take the lives and experiences of their students seriously:

> Drama is the ritualizing of imagination, and my imagination, unlike my body, is not sitting under a tree taking notes. If my body is ever to unlearn its boredom and find its ritual rhythm, it will do so dramatically. It will do so by pretending and imagining. (239)

What McLaren is calling for here is a liberating pedagogy that, in its planning, must take into account the students' instinctive ability to create. It is not surprising that he should turn to drama in his recommendations for more relevant and engaging curricula. The ritual of schooling must consider the rituals of daily living and the students' experience of popular or street culture. He describes what he sees as the basis for an enduring curriculum:

> Considering the dramatic qualities of ritual, it would appear instructive for both drama theorists and ritologists to begin to forge connections between ritual and drama applicable to the creation of improved curricular programming. Curriculum planners could also derive benefits from a dialogue with ritologists. Programming should ultimately allow solutions to be posed to practices of teachers who continue to coerce reality for students through calcified and consequently shallow forms of ritualized instruction. (139)

Ultimately, a curriculum whose organization of educational pursuits is clear and experientially open-ended will allow students to imagine and to learn in a meaningful world. This is a community-built world made possible by the teacher's well-marked objectives, objectives that are not prescriptive but that enable a creative process. Dewey (1938) describes this provocative task in the following way:

> There is incumbent upon the educator the duty of instituting a

much more intelligent, and consequently more difficult, kind of planning. He must survey the capacities and needs of the particular set of individuals with whom he is dealing and must at the same time arrange the conditions which provide the subject-matter or content for experiences that satisfy these needs and develop these capacities. The planning must be flexible enough to permit free play for individuality of experience and yet firm enough to give direction towards continuous development of power. (58)

In short, the nature of the subject determines the classification of goals. The objectives of drama education identify those skills needed by an individual, as a member of a community of 'creators,' to play out a role within that community and drive the scene forward. The implications for the 'real world' are indisputable.

Philip Phenix (1975), in 'Transcendence and the Curriculum,' suggested that 'the fashioning of new constructs is not an exceptional activity reserved for a minority of gifted persons; it is rather the normal mode of behaviour for everyone' (329). In this inclusive view of the arts in education lies the key to curriculum design. In *Art as Experience*, John Dewey (1934) long ago articulated a similar understanding of art and its role in civilization as being prefigured in the very process of living. In schools, we must, therefore, avoid the elitism that is sometimes associated with the arts and that deprives them of their connection with concrete experiences. Instead, we must continue to struggle with curriculum objectives and designs to ensure that the most expansive view of the arts and learning is reflected in our professional documents. By studying the classrooms of committed and dynamic drama educators, by engaging in reflective-teacher research, and by watching students become excited about learning, we will learn most about the best practices we currently have in the field.

Epilogue

Countless millions read books, listen to music, watch the theatre, go to the cinema. Why? To say that they seek distraction, relaxation, entertainment, is to beg the question. Why is it distracting, relaxing, entertaining to sink oneself in someone else's life and problems, to identify oneself with a painting or a piece of music or with the characters in a novel, play or film? Why do we respond to such 'unreality' as though it were reality intensified? What strange, mysterious entertainment is this? And if one answers that we want to escape from an unsatisfactory existence into a much richer one, into experience without risk, then the next question arises: why is our own existence not enough? Why this desire to fulfil our unfulfilled lives through other figures, other forms, to gaze from the darkness of an auditorium at a lighted stage where something that is only play can utterly absorb us?

Ernst Fischer, *The Necessity of Art* (1959)

Fischer, whose book was founded on the conviction that art has been, still is, and always will be necessary, warns that we are inclined to take an astonishing phenomenon too much for granted, that art reflects our infinite capacity for association, for sharing experiences and ideas. He holds that humans want to be more than individuals, that they strive toward a fullness of life that our individuality with all its limitations cheats us. Simply put, people strive towards a more comprehensible, more just world, a world that makes sense.

Arts education surely no longer needs to provide rationales for its existence. And the principles of equity in education are

now generally recognized in educational discourse. Nonetheless, Eisner (1991) reminds us that the arts and humanities have generally been neglected as a way of understanding and enhancing educational practice. Schools and universities are organized into rather insular worlds, making it difficult to move outside one's own certainties to see the truths and logic of other disciplines. Canadian writer John Ralston Saul (1993) exposes how our preoccupation with 'expertise' has been to the detriment of our progress as human beings:

> The reality is that the division of knowledge into feudal fiefdoms of expertise has made general understanding and coordinated action not simply impossible but despised and distrusted. (8)

This is worrying in the present political climate where educators and government officials battle over control of the education system and over important curriculum questions. Yet I am still hopeful about education and remain convinced that reflective practitioners, beginning with their own small world of the classroom, will have an impact on educational policy.

In their classroom research, teachers in vastly different contexts might arrive at different conclusions – ones that address the specificity of their worlds – but they can still speak the common language of reflection and analysis of practice. In my view, the real value of conclusions, in educational research, is the extent to which they open up new questions. It is not important for teachers in other classroom contexts to draw the same conclusions about the education of girls or the importance of drama education that I have drawn here. In my own single-sex setting 'voice' has been integral in understanding adolescent girls and drama education, but this quality of 'voice' will naturally change in different contexts. I would argue that the strength of reflective-teacher research is precisely in its attention to the contextualized voices, the setting, and complexities of classrooms. The strength of classroom-based research lies not only in what it says, but in who speaks; not only in what it does not say, but in who does not speak. In participant-observation inquiries, we are

well placed to make a positioned claim to truth, which is more useful, I maintain, than a position claiming universal truth.

My initial orienting question – Does drama education in a single-sex classroom engage girls' experiences and expand the perspectives available to them? – served to keep me focused when I began observing and discussing drama work with adolescent girls. I had been aware that the educational research and reports I had read on girls seemed to pathologize them and underscore their powerlessness in schools. My own experience doing drama with them told me otherwise.

Current literature on gender and education has explored the ways in which the sexes are differently gendered from the earliest years. Gender studies with a sociological perspective have looked to cultural distinctions to explain the 'differences' between the sexes. Such studies have often pointed to the advantages of single-sex education, or all-female learning environments, but have also tended to stress similarities or an 'essentialness' among girls as a group. My classroom observation of tenth-grade girls offers an important but different insight about single-sex education: when gender is 'relaxed,' other categories of identity emerge more strongly in these same-sex groupings. Our approach to equity refused to take existing understandings about the education of girls as 'fixed.' It also rejected a deficit approach to understanding girls' educational experiences.

With this in mind, I exploited drama education practices that ask students to respond to new understandings in a dialogic process within the classroom. Girls learned how to make choices, aiming for success rather than fearing failure or remaining silenced by learned helplessness. I saw that drama practices do not conceal differences but invite students to select from their experiences – the specificities of their lives – in order to rework and reframe their understandings. Single-sex drama education is a vibrant setting for girls' knowledge and girls' voices. Simply put, drama in a single-sex context draws upon the differences among girls and is propelled by the tensions and contradictions within such a diverse group.

Brown and Gilligan's (1992) study, although largely con-

ducted in middle- to upper-middle-class American settings, is significant in that it joined women's psychology with girls' development in order to learn about girls' relational knowing rather than comparing girls with boys in order to understand the differences. Their study also suggested that girls' schools, rather than diffusing girls' voices, need to allow girls to express strong feelings and work with conflict and confrontation. Conflicts in drama education become the sites for struggle and create possibilities for greater knowledge of self and other. The girls themselves are the 'subjects,' the essential content, of the fictional worlds in the creative processes of dramatic role-play. These processes are not meant to ameliorate previous exclusions of girls' perspectives in classroom activities. They are not a correction of previous understandings, but a reorientation in thinking. They constitute a creative and not a reactive stance.

At a developmental stage often marked by contradiction and conflict, doing drama provides high-school girls with opportunities to construct their worlds and their 'selves.' The aesthetic impulse to contemplate and frame the detailed workings of dramatic action makes the small loom large. Harvesting self-contradiction and encouraging a multi-perspectival view of life promote a dialectic of both questioning and self-questioning. Working with drama conventions that ask students to contract and dilate the self leads to more complex views of human beings. Avoiding clichés and searching for fresh expression allow for new ways to look at old subjects.

In my view, schools need to begin to operate with a more evolved understanding of conflict. Conflict does not need to be 'managed'; it needs to be understood. Considerable writing in the area of drama education highlights the teaching of empathy for others and the interrogation of self. Observing my students helped me confirm that understanding others leads us to a deeper and more differentiated understanding of ourselves. I remember clearly Rosa's wise words about 'being in another's shoes':

I learned that in every situation everyone views their own story as

the truth, builds up their own truth. And through acting out different points of view we understood why everyone wanted their story to be the truth.

And so in providing here a construction of our reality, a picture of our learning together – teacher-researcher and students – I trust that I have brought my own truths to this picture. The parts of myself that are 'daughter,' I think, have been among the greatest sources of strength and understanding to me. These parts have informed my teaching of, and learning from, girls in immeasurable ways. My mother's respect for life as well as my father's appetite for the celebration of things large and small have prepared me well for the privilege, responsibility, and pleasure of teaching. It is in their spirit that I have been able to conceive of possibilities, to be that voice for girls that was, at critical moments in my young life, present for me.

Heathcote (in Johnson and O'Neill, 1984) reminds us that when working with children, we must have the ability to be ourselves. Doing reflective-practitioner research asks us to look at our actions and choices in intentional and rigorous ways. As a result, it offers powerful tools for authentic teaching, professional development, and school reform. Heathcote also urged teachers to negotiate with significance in classroom relations – to live our lives in classrooms as though they really mattered. During my own research process, I was repeatedly struck by our possibilities as teachers to take real delight in our classrooms and ennoble the people in them.

References

American Association of University Women Educational Foundation. 1992. *How Schools Shortchange Girls*. Washington, DC: American Association of University Women Educational Foundation.

American Association of University Women Educational Foundation. 1998. *Single-Sex Education for Girls*. Washington, DC: American Association of University Women Educational Foundation

American Institutes for Research. 1999. *Gender Gaps: Where Schools Still Fail Our Children*. New York: Marlow and Company.

Anderson, G.L. 1989. Critical Ethnography in Education: Origins, Current Status, and New Directions. *Review of Educational Research* 59: 249–70.

Anderson, G.L., and K. Herr. 1999. The New Paradigm Wars: Is There Room for Rigorous Practitioner Knowledge in Schools and Universities? *Educational Researcher* 28(5): 12–21.

Arnot, M., and G. Weiner, eds. 1987. *Gender and the Politics of Schooling*. London: Hutchinson.

Aston, E. 1995. *An Introduction to Feminism and Theatre*. London and New York: Routledge.

Atkinson, P. 1990. *The Ethnographic Imagination: Textual Construction of Reality*. London: Routledge.

Atwell, N. 1987. *In the Middle: Writing, Reading, and Learning with Adolescents*. Portsmouth, NH: Boynton/Cook.

Avi. 1991. *Nothing But the Truth*. New York: Orchard Books

Banks, J. 1993. The Canon Debate, Knowledge Construction and Multicultural Education. *Educational Researcher* 22(5): 4–14.

Banks, J. 1994. The Historical Reconstruction of Knowledge about Race: The Implications for Transformative Teaching. Unpublished paper.

Barton, B., and D. Booth. 1990. *Stories in the Classroom*. Markham, ON: Pembroke/Heinemann Educational Books.

Bauch, P. 1989. Single-Sex Schooling and Women's Education. Paper presented at the Annual General Meeting of Catholic Education Association. Chicago.

Belsey, C. 1991. *The Subject of Tragedy: Identity and Difference in Renaissance Drama*. London and New York: Routledge.

Berger, J. 1972. *Ways of Seeing*. Harmondsworth: Penguin.

Best, D. 1985. *Feeling and Reason in the Arts*. London: George Allen and Unwin.

Blair, H., and K. Sanford. 1999, April. Single-Sex Classrooms: A Place for Transformation of Policy and Practice. Paper presented at the American Education Research Association Conference. Montreal, Quebec.

Boal, A. 1992. *Games for Actors and Non-Actors* (Adrian Jackson, Trans.). London: Routledge.

Bolton, G. 1971. Drama and Theatre in Education: A Survey. In N. Dodd and W. Hickson (Eds.), *Drama and Theatre in Education*. London: Heinemann.

Bolton, G. 1979. *Towards a Theory of Drama in Education*. London: Longman Group Ltd.

Bolton, G. 1984. *Drama as Education*. Harlow, Essex: Longman Group Ltd.

Bolton, G. 1996. Afterword: Drama as Research. In P. Taylor (Ed.), *Researching Drama and Arts Education: Paradigms and Possibilities* (pp. 187–94). London: The Falmer Press.

Booth, D. 1994. *Story Drama: Reading, Writing and Roleplaying across the Curriculum*. Toronto: Pembroke Publishers Limited.

Booth, D., and A. Martin-Smith. 1988. *Re-cognizing Richard Courtney: Selected Writings on Drama in Education*. Markham: Pembroke Publishers Ltd.

Booth, D., and C. Thornley-Hall (Eds.). 1991. Our Own Words and the Words of Others. In *The Talk Curriculum*. Markham: Pembroke Publishers Ltd.

Booth, D., and G. Wells. 1994. Developing Communities of Inquiry. *Orbit* 25(4): 23–8.

Brighton, C. 1991. *Dearest Grandmama*. London: Faber and Faber.

Brook, P. 1968. *The Empty Space*. London: McGibbon and Kee.

Brook, P. 1987. *The Shifting Point: Theatre, Film, Opera 1946–1987*. New York: Theatre Communications Group.

Brook, P. 1996. Peter Brook in Conversation with Michael Billington at the Royal Exchange Theatre, Manchester, 18 March 1994. In M. Delgado and P. Heritage (Eds.), *In Contact with the Gods: Directors Talk Theatre* (pp. 37–54). Manchester: Manchester University Press.

Brown, L., and C. Gilligan. 1992. *Meeting at the Crossroads: Women's Psychology and Girls' Development*. Cambridge and London: Harvard University Press.

Bruner, J. 1960. *The Process of Education*. Cambridge, MA: Harvard University Press.

Buege, C. 1993. The Effect of Mainstreaming on Attitude and Self-Concept Using Creative Drama and Social Skills Training. *Youth Theatre Journal* 7(3): 19–22.

Burdell, P., and B. Swadener. 1999. Critical Personal Narrative and Autoethnography in Education: Reflections on a Genre. *Educational Researcher* 28(6): 21–6.

Burrell, G., and G. Morgan. 1979. *Sociological Paradigms and Organizational Analysis*. London: Heineman Educational Books.

Cahill, S. 1975. *Women and Fiction*. New York: Penguin Books.

Canadian Teachers' Federation. 1990. *The A Capella Papers of the Canadian Teachers' Federation*. Ottawa: Canadian Teachers' Federation.

Carroll, J. 1996. Escaping the Information Abattoir: Critical and Transformative Research in Drama Classrooms. In P. Taylor (Ed.), *Researching Drama and Arts Education: Paradigms and Possibilities* (pp. 72–84). London: The Falmer Press.

Case, S.E. 1988. *Feminism and Theatre*. London: MacMillan.

Chambers, V. 1995. Betrayal Feminism. In B. Findlen (Ed.), *Listen Up: Voices from the Next Feminist Generation* (pp. 21–35). Washington: Seal Press.

Cherryholmes, C. 1988. *Power and Criticism: Post-Structuralist Investigations in Education*. New York: Teachers College Press.

Clandinin, D.J., and F.M. Connelly. 1987. Teachers' Personal Practical Knowledge: What Counts as 'Personal' in Studies of the Personal. *Journal of Curriculum Studies* 19(6): 487–500.

Clandinin, D.J., and F.M. Connelly. 1991. Narrative and Story in Practice and Research. In D. Schon (Ed.), *The Reflective Turn: Case Studies in and on Educational Research* (pp. 258–81). New York: Teachers College Press.

Clark, J., W. Dobson, T. Goode, and J. Neelands. 1997. *Lessons for the Living: Drama and the Integrated Curriculum*. Newmarket, ON: Mayfair Cornerstone Limited.

Cohen, E. 1994. *Designing Groupwork: Strategies for the Heterogeneous Classroom* (2nd ed.). New York: Teachers College Press.

Cohen, L., and L. Manion. 1994. *Research Methods in Education* (4th ed.). New York: Routledge.

Collis, B. 1987. Adolescent Females in Computers: Real and Perceived Barriers. In J. Gaskell and A. McLaren (Eds.), *Women and Education: A Canadian Perspective* (pp. 117–31). Calgary: Detselig.

Connelly, F.M., and J.D. Clandinin. 1988. *Teachers As Curriculum Planners: Narratives of Experience*. New York: Teachers College, Columbia University.

Courtney, R. 1980. *The Dramatic Curriculum*. New York: Drama Book Specialists.

Courtney, R. 1982. *Re-Play: Studies of Human Drama in Education*. Toronto: OISE Press.

Courtney, R. 1987. *Dictionary of Developmental Drama*. Springfield, IL: Chas. C. Thomas.

Courtney, R. 1989. *Play, Drama and Thought: The Intellectual Background to Dramatic Education*. Toronto: Simon and Pierre Publishing Co. Ltd.

Courtney, R. 1990. *Drama and Intelligence: A Cognitive Theory*. Montreal/ Kingston: McGill-Queen's University Press.

Crockett, L., and A. Peterson. 1987. Pubertal Status and Psychological Development: Findings from an Early Adolescent Study. In R. Lerner and T. Foch (Eds.), *Biological-Psychosocial Interactions in Early Adolescence* (pp.173–88). Hillsdale, NJ: Erlbaum.

Culley, M., and C. Portuges (Eds.). 1985. *Gendered Subjects: The Dynamics of Feminist Teaching*. Boston: Routledge and Kegan Paul.

Daley, S. 1991, January 9. Girls' Self-Esteem Is Lost on Way to Adolescence, New Study Finds. *New York Times* (National Edition): B1.

de Beauvoir, S. 1959. *Memoirs of a Dutiful Daughter*. Harmondsworth: Penguin.

Dei, G.J.S. 1993. The Challenges of Anti-Racist Education in Canada. *Canadian Ethnic Studies* 25(2): 36–50.

Dei, G.J.S. 1994. Reflections of an Anti-Racist Pedagogue. In L. Erwin and P. MacLennan (Eds.), *Sociology of Education in Canada: Critical Perspectives on Theory, Research and Practice* (pp. 290–310). Toronto: Copp Clark Pitman.

Delamont, S. 1990. *Sex Roles and the School*. London: Routledge.

Delamont, S., and D. Hamilton. 1986. Revisiting Classroom Research: A Continuing Cautionary Tale. In M. Hammersley (Ed.), Controversies in Classroom Research (pp. 25–43). Milton Keynes, England/Philadelphia: Open University Press.

Delpit, L. 1988. The Silenced Dialogue: Power and Pedagogy in Educating Other People's Children. *Harvard Educational Review* 58(3): 280–98.

Dewey, J. 1926, 1916. *Democracy and Education: An Introduction to the Philosophy of Education*. New York: Macmillan.

Dewey, J. 1934. *Art as Experience*. New York: Milton, Balch.

Dewey, J. 1938. *Experience and Education*. New York: MacMillan.

Dickens, N. 1995. Collectively Created Theatre: Guiding and Supporting the Creative Process. Workshop at Young People's Theatre, Toronto.

Dodd, N., and W. Hickson (Eds.). 1971. *Drama and Theatre in Education*. London: Heinemann.

Dolan, J. 1988. *The Feminist Spectator as Critic*. Ann Arbor: University of Michigan Press.

Doyle, C. 1989. *A Site for Critical Pedagogy.* St. John's: Publications Committee, Faculty of Education, Memorial University of Newfoundland.

Doyle, C. 1993. *Raising Curtains on Education: Drama as a Site for Critical Pedagogy.* Westport, CT: Bergin and Garvey.

Draper, D. 1993. We're Back with Gobbo: The Re-establishment of Gender Relations Following a School Merger. In P. Woods and M. Hammersley (Eds.), *Gender and Ethnicity in Schools: Ethnographic Accounts* (pp. 49–62). New York: Routledge.

Edmiston, B., and J. Wilhelm. 1996. Playing the Different Keys: Research Notes for Action Researchers and Reflective Drama Practitioners. In P. Taylor (Ed.), *Researching Drama and Arts Education: Paradigms and Possibilities* (pp. 89–96). London: The Falmer Press.

Eisner, E. (Ed.). 1971. *Confronting Curriculum Reform.* Boston: Little, Brown.

Eisner, E. (Ed.). 1976. *The Arts, Human Development and Education.* Berkeley, CA: McCutchan Publishing.

Eisner, E. 1991. *The Enlightened Eye: Qualitative Inquiry and the Enhancement of Educational Practice.* New York: Macmillan.

Elliot, J. 1974. Sex Role Constraints on Freedom of Discussion: A Neglected Reality of the Classroom. *The New Era* 55(6): 147–55.

Feagin, J., A. Orum, and G. Sjoberg (Eds.). 1991. *A Case for the Case Study.* Chapel Hill and London: The University of North Carolina.

Feldhendler, D. 1994. Augusto Boal and Jacob L. Moreno: Theatre and Therapy. In M. Shutzman and J. Cohen-Cruz (Eds.), *Playing Boal: Theatre, Therapy, Activism* (pp. 87–109). London: Routledge

Fetterman, D. 1984. Doing Ethnographic Educational Evaluation. In D. Fetterman (Ed.), *Ethnography in Educational Evaluation* (pp. 13–19). Beverly Hills: Sage Publications.

Fischer, E. 1959. *The Necessity of Art: A Marxist Approach* (Anna Bostock, Trans.). Harmondsworth: Penguin Books.

Forman, F. 1990. *Feminism and Education: A Canadian Perspective.* Toronto: OISE, Centre for Women's Studies in Education.

Foucault, M. 1980. *Power/Knowledge.* New York: Pantheon Books.

Fowler, C. 1994. Strong Arts, Strong Schools. In *Educational Leadership.* Article commissioned by the Getty Center for Education in the Arts, extracted from Charles Fowler's keynote address at ASCD's Annual Conference, Chicago.

Freire, P. 1972. *Pedagogy of the Oppressed.* England: Penguin Books.

Freire, P. 1998a. *Teachers as Cultural Workers: Letters to Those Who Dare Teach.* New York: Westview Press.

Freire, P. 1998b. *Pedagogy of Freedom: Ethics, Democracy, and Civic Courage.* Lanham, MD: Rowman and Littlefield Publishers.

Friedman, M., and C. Crawford Cousins. 1996. Holding the Space: Gender, Race and Conflict in Training. In S. Walters and L. Manicom (Eds.), *Gender in Popular Education: Methods for Empowerment* (pp. 61–86). London: Zed Books.

Fuchs, A. 1990. *Playing the Market: The Market Theatre in Johannesburg 1976–1986*. Chur, Switzerland: Larwood Academic Publishers.

Fuller, M. 1985. Black Girls in a London Comprehensive School. In P. Woods and M. Hammersley (Eds.), *Life in School: The Sociology of Pupil Culture* (pp. 77–88). Milton Keynes, England: Open University Press.

Fuss, D. 1989. *Essentially Speaking*. New York: Routledge.

Gallas, K. 1994. *The Languages of Learning: How Children Talk, Write, Dance, Draw, and Sing Their Understanding of the World*. New York: Teachers College Press.

Gardner, H. 1983. *Frames of Mind: The Theory of Multiple Intelligences*. New York: Basic Books.

Gaskell, J. 1985. Course Enrollment in the High School: The Perspective of Working-Class Females. *Sociology of Education* 58(1): 48–59.

Gaskell, J., and A. McClaren (Eds.). 1987. *Women and Education: A Canadian Perspective*. Calgary, AB: Detselig.

Gaskell, J., A. McClaren, and M. Novogrodsky. 1989. *Claiming an Education: Feminism and Canadian Schools*. Toronto: Our Schools/Ourselves Education Foundation.

Gaskell, J., and J. Willinsky (Eds.). 1995. *Gender In/forms Curriculum: From Enrichment to Transformation*. New York: Teachers College Press.

Ghetty Center for Education in the Arts. 1985. *Beyond Creating ... The Place for Art in America's Schools*. Los Angeles: J. Paul Ghetty Trust, Ghetty Center for Education in the Arts.

Gilligan, C. 1982. *In a Different Voice: Psychological Theory and Women's Development*. Cambridge, MA: Harvard University Press.

Gilligan, C. 1990. Teaching Shakespeare's Sister: Notes from the Underground of Female Adolescence. In C. Gilligan, N. Lyons, and T. Hanmer (Eds.), *Making Connections: The Relational Worlds of Adolescent Girls at Emma Willard School* (pp. 6–29). Cambridge and London: Harvard University Press.

Giroux, H. 1981. Toward a New Sociology of Curriculum. In H. Giroux, A. Penna, and W. Pinar (Eds.), *Curriculum and Instruction: Alternatives in Education* (pp. 98–108). Berkeley, CA: McCutchan Publishing.

Gourgey, A., J. Bosseau, and J. Delagado. 1985. The Impact of an Improvisational Dramatics Program on Student Attitudes and Achievement. *Children's Theatre Review* 34(3): 9–14.

Green, J. 1990. *Morning of Her Day*. London: Darf Publishers.

Greene, M. 1978. *Landscapes of Learning*. New York: Teachers College Press.

Greene, M. 1991. Foreword. In C. Witherell and N. Noddings (Eds.), *Stories Lives Tell: Narrative and Dialogue in Education* (pp. ix–xi)). New York and London: Teachers College, Columbia University.

Greene, M. 1996. Foreword. In P. Taylor (Ed.), *Researching Drama and Arts Education: Paradigms and Possibilities*. London: The Falmer Press.

Grugeon, E. 1993. Gender Implications of Children's Playground Culture. In P. Woods and M. Hammersley (Eds.), *Gender and Ethnicity in Schools: Ethnographic Accounts* (pp. 29–44). New York: Routledge.

Grumet, M. 1988. *Bitter Milk: Women and Teaching*. Amherst: The University of Massachusetts Press.

Grumet, M. 1989. Feminism and the Phenomenology of the Familiar. In G. Milburn, I. Goodson, and R. Clark (Eds.), *Re-interpreting Curriculum Research: Images and Arguments* (pp. 87–101). London, ON. The Althouse Press.

Grumet, M. 1991. The Politics of Personal Knowledge. In C. Witherell and N. Noddings (Eds.), *Stories Lives Tell: Narrative and Dialogue in Education* (pp. 67–77). New York and London: Teachers College, Columbia University.

Grumet, M., and W. Pinar. 1976. *Toward a Poor Curriculum*. Dubuque, IA: Kendall/Hunt.

Harste, J. 1993. Inquiry-Based Instruction. In *Primary Voices K–6* 1(2): 2–5. Urbana, IL: National Council of Teachers of English.

Harste, J., K. Short, and C. Burke. 1988. *Creating Classrooms for Authors: The Reading Writing Connections*. Portsmouth NH: Heinemann.

Hawthorne, J. 1992. *A Concise Glossary of Contemporary Literary Theory*. London: Edward Arnold.

Heathcote, D. 1984a. Drama as a Process for Change. In L. Johnson and C. O'Neill (Eds.), *Collected Writings on Education and Drama* (pp. 114–25). Evanston, IL: Northwestern University Press.

Heathcote, D. 1984b. Excellence in Teaching. In L. Johnson and C. O'Neill (Eds.), *Collected Writings on Education and Drama* (pp. 18–25). Evanston, IL: Northwestern University Press.

Heathcote, D. 1984c. Drama and Education: Subject or System? In L. Johnson and C. O'Neill (Eds.), *Collected Writings on Education and Drama* (pp. 61–79). Evanston, IL: Northwestern University Press.

Herst, B. 1991. A Woman's Comedy. In A. Wilson (Ed.), *Canadian Theatre Review* (Winter): 63–86.

Hileman, L. 1985. Exploring Drama with Emotionally Disturbed Adolescents. *Pointer* 30(1): 12–15.

hooks, b. 1994a. *Teaching to Transgress: Education as the Practice of Freedom*. New York: Routledge.

hooks, b. 1994b. *Outlaw Culture: Resisting Representations*. New York: Routledge.

Hundert, D.A. 1996. *Paths of Learning through 'The Forest of Dreams': Senior Secondary Students and Theatre for Young Audiences.* Doctoral dissertation, University of Toronto, 1996.

Hycner, R.H. 1985. Some Guidelines for the Phenomenological Analysis of Interview Data. *Human Studies* 8: 279–303.

Isaacs, S. 1993. *Intellectual Growth in Young Children.* London: Routledge.

Johnson, L., and C. O'Neill (Eds.). 1984. *Dorothy Heathcote: Collected Writings on Education and Drama.* Evanston, IL: Northwestern University Press.

Junell, J.S. 1974. Is Rational Man Our First Priority? In E. Eisner and E. Vallence (Eds.), *Conflicting Conceptions of Curriculum* (pp. 106–16). Stanford: McCutchan Publishers Corp.

Kaufman, I. 1971. The Art of Curriculum Making in the Arts. In E. Eisner (Ed.), *Confronting Curriculum Reform* (pp. 91–112). Boston: Little, Brown and Company.

Kazemeck, F. 1995. Reading and the Female Moral Imagination: 'Words Mean More than What Is Set Down on Paper.' In J. Gaskell and J. Willinsky (Eds.), *Gender In/forms Curriculum: From Enrichment to Transformation* (pp. 77–95). New York: Teachers College Press.

Kenway, J., and S. Willis (Eds.). 1990. *Hearts and Minds: Self-Esteem and the Schooling of Girls.* London: Falmer.

Kessler, S., D. Ashenden, B. Connell, and G. Dowsett. 1987. Gender Relations in Secondary Schooling. In M. Arnot and G. Weiner (Eds.), *Gender and the Politics of Schooling* (pp. 223–36). London: Hutchinson.

Lepage, R. 1996. In Conversation with Alison McAlpine, at Le Café du Monde, Quebec City, 17 February 1995. In M. Delgado and P. Heritage (Eds.), *In Contact With the Gods? Directors Talk Theatre* (pp. 129–57). Manchester and New York: Manchester University Press.

Lips, H. 1987. Education and the Status of Women: A Challenge for Teachers. In L. Stewin and J. McCann (Eds.), *Contemporary Educational Issues: The Canadian Mosaic* (pp. 298–314). Toronto: Copp Clark Pitman.

Locke, A. 1928. Art or Propaganda? In N. Huggins (Ed.), *Voices from the Harlem Renaissance* (pp. 309–21). New York: Oxford University Press, 1976.

Mac an Ghaill, M. 1993. Beyond the White Norm: The Use of Qualitative Methods in the Study of Black Youths' Schooling in England. In P. Woods and M. Hammersley (Eds.), *Gender and Ethnicity in Schools: Ethnographic Accounts* (pp. 142–60). New York: Routledge.

McCammon, L.A. 1995. Commentary on 'Reflective Practice and Drama Research' and 'Our Adventure of Experiencing.' *Youth Theatre Journal* 9: 45–8.

McGrath, J. 1981. *A Good Night Out: Popular Theatre, Audience, Class and Form.* London: Nick Hern Books.

McLaren, P. 1986. *Schooling as a Ritual Performance*. London: Routledge and Kegan Paul.

McClaren, P. 1995. Collisions with Otherness: 'Traveling' Theory, Postcolonial Criticism, and the Politics of Ethnographic Practice – The Mission of the Wounded Ethnographer. In P. McClaren and J. Giarelli (Eds.), *Critical Theory and Educational Research* (pp. 271–300). New York: State University of New York Press.

Metropolitan Separate School Board. 1989. *Dramatic Arts Core Curriculum for Secondary Schools*. Toronto: Metropolitan Separate School Board.

Millard, E. 1997. *Differently Literate: Boys, Girls and the Schooling of Literacy*. London: The Falmer Press.

Miller, J. 1988. *The Holistic Curriculum*. Toronto: OISE Press.

Ministry of Education and Training. 1999. *The Ontario Curriculum. Grades 9 and 10: The Arts*. Toronto: Queen's Printer for Ontario.

Mishler, E. 1986. *Research Interviewing: Context and Narrative*. Cambridge: Harvard University Press.

Mobley, J. 1979. *Starhusband*. New York: Doubleday.

Mohanty, C.T. 1990. On Race and Voice: Challenges for Liberal Education in the 1990s. *Cultural Critique* 14: 179–207.

Monaco, N., and E. Gaier. 1992. Single-Sex versus Coeducational Environment and Achievement in Adolescent Females. *Adolescence* 27: 579–94.

Moore, S. 1984. *The Stanislavski System: The Professional Training of an Actor*. New York: Penguin Books.

Morgan, N., and J. Saxton. 1987. *Teaching Drama: A Mind of Many Wonders*. London: Hutchinson.

Nagy, P. 1993. Education as Harvesting: Drama in Education as Tender Fruit. *Canadian Journal of Education* 18(2): 117–31.

Neelands, J. 1984. *Making Sense of Drama: A Guide to Classroom Practice*. London: Heinemann Educational in association with 2D Magazine.

Neelands, J. 1990. *Structuring Drama Work: A Handbook of Available Forms in Theatre and Drama*. Cambridge: Cambridge University Press.

Neelands, J. 1992. *Learning through Imagined Experience*. London: Hodder and Stoughton.

Neelands, J. 1996. Reflections from an Ivory Tower: Towards an Interactive Research Paradigm. In P. Taylor (Ed.), *Researching Drama and Arts Education: Paradigms and Possibilities* (pp. 156–66). London: Falmer Press.

O'Neill, C. 1995. *Drama Worlds: A Framework for Process Drama*. Portsmouth, NH: Heinemann.

O'Neill, C., and A. Lambert. 1982. *Drama Structures: A Practical Handbook for Teachers*. London: Stanley Thornes.

Ontario Ministry of Education. 1981. *Dramatic Arts: Intermediate Senior.* Toronto: Ministry of Education.

Orenstein, P. 1994. *School Girls: Young Women, Self-Esteem, and the Confidence Gap.* New York: Doubleday.

Orum, A., J. Feagin, and G. Sjoberg. 1991. *A Case for the Case Study.* Chapel Hill and London: The University of North Carolina.

Payne, I. 1980. A Working Class Girl in a Grammar School. In G. Weiner and E. Sarah (Eds.), *Learning to Lose* (pp. 12–31). London: The Womens' Press.

Peterson, P.L., and E. Fennema. 1985. Effective Teaching, Student Engagement in Classroom Activities, and Sex-Related Differences. *American Educational Research Journal* 22(3): 309–35.

Phenix, P. 1975. Transcendance and the Curriculum. In W. Pinar (Ed.), *Curriculum Theorizing* (pp. 321–37). Berkeley, CA: McCutchan Publishing.

Piaget, J. 1971. *Structuralism.* London: Routledge and Kegan Paul.

Piaget, J., and B. Inhelder. 1975. Adolescent Thinking. In J. Sants and H.J. Butcher (Eds.), *Developmental Psychology: Selected Readings* (pp. 79–121). Harmondsworth/Baltimore: Penguin Books.

Pinar, W. (Ed.). 1975. Currerre: Toward Reconceptualization. In *Curriculum Theorizing: The Reconceptualists* (pp. 43–59). Berkeley, CA: McCutchan Publishing.

Pinar, W. 1981. The Reconceptualization of Curriculum Studies. In H. Giroux, A. Penna, and W. Pinar (Eds.), *Curriculum and Instruction: Alternatives in Education* (pp. 87–97). Berkeley, CA: McCutchan Publishing.

Pitman, W. 1998. *Learning the Arts in an Age of Uncertainty.* Toronto: Aylmer Express Limited.

Powers, J.B. 1992. *The 'Girl Question' in Education.* Washington, DC: Falmer.

Pratt. D. 1987. The Owl, the Rose and the Big Bang: Curriculum Options for the 21st Century. In L. Stewin and J. McCann (Eds.), *Contemporary Educational Issues: The Canadian Mosaic* (pp. 610–27). Toronto: Copp Clark Pitman.

Rich, A. 1979. Women and Honour: Some Notes on Lying. In A. Rich (Ed.), *On Lies, Secrets and Silence* (pp. 23–31). New York: W.W. Norton.

Roach Pierson, R. 1991. Experience, Difference, Dominance and Voice in the Writing of Canadian Women's History. In K. Offen, R. Roach Pierson, and J. Rendall (Eds.), *Writing Women's History: International Perspectives* (pp. 79–106). London: Macmillan Bloomington.

Rosenberg, H. 1987. *Creative Drama and Imagination: Transforming Ideas into Action.* New York: Holt, Rineheart and Winston.

Ross, C. 1988. Drama Ground: Premises and Promises. *Language Arts* 65(1): 41–4.

Ross, M. 1984. *The Aesthetic Impulse*. Oxford: Pergamon Press.

Ross, M. 1985. *The Aesthetic in Education*. Oxford: Pergamon Press.

Russel, T., and H. Munby. 1991. Reframing: The Role of Experience in Developing Teachers' Professional Knowledge. In D. Schon (Ed.), *The Reflective Turn: Case Studies in and on Educational Research* (pp. 164–87). New York: Teachers College Press.

Sadker, M., and Sadker, D. 1994. *Failing at Fairness: How America's Schools Cheat Girls*. Toronto: Maxwell MacMillan International.

Salutin, R. 1997, March 21. Search and Reflection Give Value on the Journey. *The Globe and Mail*, p. D1.

Sarah, E., M. Scott, and D. Spender. 1988. The Education of Feminists: The Case for Single-Sex Schools. In D. Spender and E. Sarah (Eds.), *Learning to Lose*, 2nd rev. ed. (pp. 55–66). London: The Women's Press

Saul, J.R. 1993. *Voltaire's Bastards: The Dictatorship of Reason in the West*. Toronto: Penguin Books.

Schon, D. 1983. *The Reflective Practitioner: How Professionals Think in Action*. New York: Basic Books.

Schon, D. (Ed.). 1991. *The Reflective Turn: Case Studies in and on Educational Practice*. New York: Columbia University Teachers College.

Schubert, W. 1991. Teacher Lore: A Basis for Understanding Praxis. In C. Witherell and N. Noddings (Eds.), *Stories Lives Tell: Narrative and Dialogue in Education* (pp. 207–33). New York and London: Columbia University, Teachers College.

Schutzman, M. 1994. Canadian Roundtable. In M. Schutzman and J. Cohen-Cruz (Eds.), *Playing Boal: Theatre, Therapy, Activism* (pp. 198–226). London: Routledge.

Sjoberg, G., N. Williams, R. Vaughan, and A. Sjoberg. 1991. The Case Study Approach in Social Research: Basic Methodological Issues. In J. Feagin, A. Orum, G. Sjoberg (Eds.), *A Case for the Case Study* (pp. 1–26). Chapel Hill and London: The University of North Carolina.

Skelton, C. 1993. Women and Education. In D. Richardson and V. Robinson (Eds.), *Thinking Feminist: Key Concepts in Women's Studies* (pp. 324–49). New York: The Guilford Press.

Smith, D. 1987a. An Analysis of Ideological Structures and How Women Are Excluded: Considerations for Academic Women. In J. Gaskell and A. McLaren (Eds.), *Women and Education: A Canadian Perspective* (pp. 245–62). Calgary: Detselig.

Smith, D. 1987b. *The Everyday World as Problematic*. Boston: Northeastern University Press.

Spender, D. 1982. *Invisible Women: The Schooling Scandal*. London: Writers and Readers Press.

Spender, D. 1985. *For the Record: The Meaning and Making of Feminist Knowledge*. London: The Women's Press Ltd.

Starratt, R.J. 1990. *The Drama of Schooling/The Schooling of Drama*. London: The Falmer Press.

Steinburg, S.B., and J.L. Kincheloe. 1998. *Students as Researchers: Creating Classrooms that Matter*. London: Falmer Press.

Stenhouse, L. 1971. The Humanities Curriculum Project: The Rationale. *Theory into Practice* 10: 154–62.

Stenhouse, L. 1975. *An Introduction to Curriculum Research and Development*. London: Heinemann.

Stoppard, T. 1995. *Conversations with Stoppard*. London: N. Hern.

Straus, E. 1991. *Drama and Generic Skills: The Movement of Skills from the Drama Class to the Workplace*. Thesis. Toronto: Ontario Institute for Studies in Education.

Taussig, M., and R. Schechner. 1994. Boal in Brazil, France, the USA: An Interview with Augusto Boal. In M. Schutzman and J. Cohen-Cruz (Eds.), *Playing Boal: Theatre, Therapy, Activism* (pp. 17–32). London: Routledge.

Taylor, P. 1995. Wanting More or Demanding Less? A Response to McCammon. *Youth Theatre Journal* 9: 19–28.

Taylor, P. 1996. Doing Reflective Practitioner Research in Arts Education. In P. Taylor (Ed.), *Researching Drama and Arts Education: Paradigms and Possibilities* (pp. 1–21). London: The Falmer Press.

Thompson, A. 1997. For: Anti-Racist Education. *Curriculum Inquiry* 27(1): 7–44.

Tomkins, G., M. Connolly, and J. Bernier. 1981. *Abstract of State of the Art Review of Research in Curriculum and Instruction*. Funded by SSHRCC. Toronto: OISE.

Wagner, J. 1986. *The Search for Signs of Intelligent Life in the Universe*. New York: Harper and Row.

Walkerdine, V. 1990. *Schoolgirl Fictions*. London: Verso.

Ward, J.V. 1990. Racial Identity Formation and Transformation. In C. Gilligan, N. Lyons, and T. Hanmer (Eds.), *Making Connections: The Relational World of Adolescent Girls at Emma Willard School* (pp. 215–32). Cambridge and London: Harvard University Press.

Warner, C. 1997. The Edging in of Engagement: Exploring the Nature of Engagement in Drama. *Research in Drama Education* 2(1): 21–42.

Weiler, K. 1988. *Women Teaching for Change: Gender, Class and Power*. New York: Bergin and Garvey Publishers.

Weiler, K. 1991. Freire and a Feminist Pedagogy of Difference. *Harvard Educa-tional Review* 61(4): 449–79.

Weiner, G. 1985. *Just a Bunch of Girls.* London: Methuen.

Wells, G. 1987. *The Meaning Makers: Children Learning Language and Using Language to Learn.* London: Hodder and Stoughton.

Wells, G. 1994. *Changing Schools from Within: Creating Communities of Inquiry.* Toronto: OISE Press.

Wells, G., and G.L. Chang-Wells. 1992. *Constructing Knowledge Together: Classrooms as Centres of Inquiry and Literacy.* Portsmouth, NH: Heinemann.

Wilshire, B. 1991. *Role-Playing and Identity: The Limits of Theatre as Metaphor.* Bloomington and Indianapolis: Indiana University Press.

Winnicott, D.W. 1971. *Playing and Reality.* London: Tavistock Publications.

Winston, J. 1996. Emotion, Reason and Moral Engagement in Drama. *Research in Drama Education* 1(2): 189–200.

Wolcott, H. 1990. On Seeking – and Rejecting – Validity in Qualitative Research. In E. Eisner and A. Peshkin (Eds.), *Qualitative Inquiry in Education: The Continuing Debate.* New York: Teachers College Press.

Woods, P. 1986. *Inside Schools: Ethnography in Educational Research.* London: Routledge and Kegan Paul.

Woolf, V. 1966. *Three Guineas.* New York: A Harbinger Book, Harcourt, Brace and World.

Wright, C. 1993. Social Processes – An Ethnographic Study. In P. Woods and M. Hammersley (Eds.), *Gender and Ethnicity in Schools: Ethnographic Accounts* (pp. 213–26). New York: Routledge.

Index

adolescence, 9–10, 21, 25, 107; ambiguities of, 11, 47, 103, 132, 134; and identity, xiv, 45, 81, 85, 106, 107, 133; and self-esteem, 34–5, 45, 95, 100, 102–3, 123; and sex-role stereotypes, 32; and social 'issues,' 86, 89, 101. *See also* co-educational settings

aestheticism. *See* drama, and aesthetic learning

American Association of University Women Educational Foundation, 32, 37

American Institutes for Research, 29; *Gender Gaps: Where Schools Still Fail Our Children*, 29

Anderson and Herr, 15

art, 43, 51; in education, xi, 120; making of, xi, 102, 125, 131; metaphor in, 6, 24, 49, 78, 126

arts, 4, 6, 21, 22, 27, 107, 108, 110, 129, 131–2; and educational outcomes, 103, 121, 127; and learning theory, 21, 25, 52, 108, 126, 129

'as if,' 56, 58, 70; gesture of, xi

assessment, ix; in the arts, 11, 108, 109, 126–7; in drama education, 108–10, 121–6. *See also* arts, and educational outcomes

Atwell, N., 13

Avi, 62; *Nothing But the Truth*, 62, 102

Barton and Booth, 48, 49

Behn, A., 3, 6

Best, D., 116

Blair and Sanford, 29

Boal, A., 5

Bolton, G., xi, 47, 113, 116, 120

Booth, D., xi, 67–8

Booth and Thornley-Hall, 118

Booth and Wells, 14

Brecht, B., 83

Brighton, C., 68; *Dearest Grandmama*, 68

Brook, P., 27

Brown and Gilligan, 19, 133

Burdell and Swadener, 14

Burrell and Morgan, 107

Canadian Teachers' Federation, 32

Catholic schools, 101, 103

Cherryholmes C., 33

co-educational settings, 23, 29, 31, 77,

93; judgment in, 93–7. *See also* public education
Collis, B., 31
conflict, 133–4
constructivism, ix, 118, 126
courage, 9; of girls, 86, 100. *See also* adolescence, and self-esteem
Courtney, R., 48, 49, 55–6, 58, 107, 119, 120, 124, 126; *Re-Play: Studies of Human Drama in Education*, 120
curriculum, xi, 106, 119, 122; and constructivist theory, x, 128; in drama, 61, 76, 119, 121, 125; and gender, 28–9; individualization of, xi, 34, 129
curriculum reforms, 11; in Ontario, 108
curriculum studies, 104, 105, 128, 129

Daley, S., 34
daughter, 7, 135
death, 8, 82
de Beauvoir, S., 43; *Memoirs of a Dutiful Daughter*, 43
Delamont, S., 31
democracy, xi; and education, x, 30, 76, 102, 107, 127
Dewey, J., xi, 21, 119, 121, 128–9; *Art as Experience*, 129
diversity: and racism, 87, 88, 101. *See also* experiences of schooling, racial and ethnic affiliation in; gender, and race; single-sex schools, and diversity
Dobson, W., 52
Doyle, C., 115
drama: and aesthetic learning, 11, 21 24, 25, 48, 83, 125, 134; affective learning in, x, 4, 10, 16, 47, 51, 101, 120–1, 127; collective processes in, 25, 51, 54, 68–70, 73–4, 99, 118; constructing identities in, 55, 65; constructing 'truths' in, 50, 63; discipline of, 4, 14, 40, 119; as a gendered subject, 5; and girls' development, 6, 100, 102, 103; and intelligence, 10, 55–6, 58, 120; and moral development, 52, 59–60, 87–8; and teaching, xi, 76–7. *See also* girls, perceptions of; learning, engagement in
drama education: and curriculum development 4, 35, 77, 116, 119, 120, 127; and ideology, 82–3; research in, 3, 119
dramatic source, 44, 78
Draper, D., 35

Edmiston and Wilhelm, 110
educational theory, 14; and research, 104. *See also* curriculum studies
Eisner, E., 105, 107, 111, 132
Elliot, J., 22
ethnography in classrooms, 13–14, 18, 111
experiences of schooling, 10, 16, 98, 127–8, 133; racial and ethnic affiliation in, 91, 102

father, 6–9, 78, 117
Feagin, Orum, and Sjoberg, 110
feminism(s): and experience, 19, 33; and heterosexism, 78–9; and girls' emancipation, 37, 78, 114; theoretical discourses of, 28, 31, 33. *See also* gender
Fischer, E., 131; *The Necessity of Art: A Marxist Approach*, 131
Fowler, C., 21; 'Strong Arts, Strong Schools,' 21

Freire, P., xi, 17, 18, 20, 44, 103, 107, 117
Friedman and Crawford Cousins, 30

Gallas, K., 21
Gardner, H., 56
Gaskell, J., 28
Gaskell and McClaren, 32
Gaskell, McClaren, and Novogrodsky, 28
Gaskell and Willinsky, 28
gender, 71, 106; and assessment, 29; and classroom discursive practices, 77; conceptions of, 22, 28, 83, 106, 133; and power, 22, 27, 36, 77, 97, 114, 133; and race, 81, 89–92, 101–2, 114. *See also* adolescence, and identity
Gilligan, C. 28
girls, perceptions of, 3, 14, 28, 134. *See also* adolescence, and identity
Green, J., 46
Greene, M., 14, 85, 108
Grugeon, E., 34
Grumet, M., ix–xi, 28, 111, 119; *Bitter Milk: Women and Teaching*, 119

Hawthorne, J., 105
Heathcote, D., xi, 18, 62, 113, 114, 116, 120, 135; *Excellence in Teaching*, 113
Herst, B., 3
hooks, b., 6
humanity, xi, 61, 108; dramatic explorations of, 5, 22, 126
Hundert, D.A., 110

imagination, 4, 34, 49, 111; and learning, x, 55, 107, 116, 124, 128
improvisation, x, 10–11, 27; and dramatic action, 44, 58, 63, 118; and

risk, 54, 88, 118; and spontaneity, 55, 61, 68. *See also* role-playing
inner-city schools, 20, 38, 128
interviewing, 16, 18–29, 111; and personal narrative, 85
Issacs, S., 107

Junell, J.S., 127

Kaufman, I., 21, 105, 108
Kazemeck, F., 34
knowledge, 106, 132–3; cultural, 27, 89, 90, 100–2 114, 115; embodied, 59, 101, 115; and empathy, x, 16, 50, 118, 134; hierarchy of, 4; practitioner, 15, 44

learning: and agency, 20, 115, 118; categories (areas) of, 43–5, 76; engagement in, 9, 24, 55, 70, 73, 80; lifelong, 6, 13, 124; and meaning-making, 10, 14, 68, 76, 114, 118, 120
Lepage, R., 27
Lips, H., 36

Market Theatre of Johannesburg, 5
McGrath, J., 5
McLaren, P., 127–8
Metropolitan Separate School Board, Dramatic Arts Core Curriculum for Secondary Schools, 124
Millard, E., 75, 77
Mobley, Jane, 77; *Starhusband*, 77, 102
Monaco and Gaier, 35
Morgan and Saxton, 70; *Taxonomy of Personal Engagement*, 70
mother, 8, 78, 80–1, 135

Nagy, P., 121

Neelands, J., xi, 14, 48, 49, 52, 54, 62, 64, 75, 76, 78, 79

O'Neill, C., xi, 5, 25, 52, 107
Ontario Ministry of Education, 40, 122

pedagogy: of drama, 11; and learning theory, x, 116–17, 126, 128
Phenix, P., 129; 'Transcendence and the Curriculum,' 129
Piaget, J., ix,
Piaget and Inhelder, 107
Pitman, W., 4, 25, 52, 124, 125, 126, 127
Pratt, D., 108
public education, ix, 5; and equity, 10, 35–36, 114. See also single-sex schools

reflective-practitioner research, 10–11, 13–15, 28, 41, 85, 103, 105, 110–11, 129, 132, 135; challenges in, 17, 105, 106; participant observation in, 16, 17, 85, 104, 132–3; spontaneity in, 14, 116; videography in, 14, 16, 43, 97, 104
role-playing, 10, 27, 50, 59, 69, 74, 118, 124; and reflection, 50–1, 58–9, 76; stereoptypes in, 74–6, 83, 134; and writing, 50, 57, 66–7, 71–2, 77, 80–1, 111. See also improvisation
Ross, C., 120
Ross, M., 24–5
Russel and Munby, 15

Sadker and Sadker, 29, 32
Sarah, Scott, and Spender, 29, 32
Saul, J.R., 132
Schon, D., 15
secondary education in Ontario, 4, 51, 124

silencing: of girls' voices, 96, 133; of women's voices, 3. See also co-educational settings, judgment in
single-sex schools, 9, 29, 35–6, 97, 132–4; and diversity, 37–8, 100, 101, 133; and drama, 19, 71, 103, 104, 132–3; and gender equity, 3, 23, 29, 30–1, 93–4, 106, 133. See also democracy, and education
Skelton, C., 31
Smith, D., 32–4, 53
specificity, 9, 132–3
Spender, D., 31, 36; Invisible Women – The Schooling Scandal, 36
Starratt, R.J., 114
Steinburg and Kinchloe, 9
Stenhouse, L., 106
St Jude's College School, 38–41, 91, 100–2
Stoppard, T., 58
story-telling, 10, 23, 43, 79
Straus, E., 127; 'Drama and Generic Skills: The Movement of Skills from the Drama Class to the Workplace,' 127
subjectivity, xi, 32–3, 78, 106. See also feminism(s), theoretical discourses of

Taylor, P., 14, 110; Researching Drama and Arts Education: Paradigms and Possibilities, 85
teachers: drama, 44, 47, 114, 116, 124; education of, ix, 44; equity-centred, 10, 97; expertise of, xi, 9, 113, 114, 115, 116–17, 118; -in-role, 55, 68, 114
teaching: and freedom, 6; creating possibilities through, 6, 7, 44, 115, 135; and passion, xi, 117; roles, 5,

106, 114, 117. *See also* reflective-practitioner research

tension(s), 43, 107; between perspectives, 47, 53, 60, 71, 75–6, 102, 133; in role-playing, 51, 134. *See also* diversity; gender

theatre: art of, 49; conventions of, 47, 51, 54, 62–3, 68–9, 79, 101, 125; and drama, 24; and humanity, 5

theatre of the oppressed, 5

Tomkins, Connolly, and Bernier, 104

urban schooling, 10; in Canada, 10, 72; and diversity, 20; 38. *See also* inner-city schools

Wagner, J., 73; *The Search for Signs of Intelligent Life in the Universe*, 73

Walkerdine, V., 77

Warner, C., 70

Weiler, K., 114

Wells, G., 77

Wells and Chang-Wells, 115, 118

"what happens when,' x, 45, 47, 74, 75

Wilshire, B., 107

Winnicot, D.W., 107

Wolcott, H.F., 104

Young People's Theatre, 52